The
BikeBOOK

7th Edition

Complete bicycle maintenance

James Witts and Mark Storey

Contents

CHOOSING
A BIKE

Adult bikes

Before buying a bike, ask yourself – what type of riding do you intend to do? Many a bicycle has been purchased in haste on the first sunny day of spring, only to lie unused in garages and gardens throughout the country as their owners realise they bought the wrong size or style of bike. If you're new to cycling, consider borrowing or hiring a bike before spending your hard-earned money buying one.

For many years the adult bike market was dominated by 27in (700c) wheeled road bikes. The rise of the 26in-wheeled mountain bike in the mid-1970s challenged that dominance and mountain-bike sales soon outnumbered those of traditional adult bikes. In recent years we've seen an increase in so-called hybrid bikes (often called 'city bikes' or 'commuter bikes') with heavy-duty 700c wheels and tyres. (See the appendix at the back of this book for an explanation of tyre and wheel sizes.) Added to the mix, we now have 29in-wheeled mountain bikes, fat bikes and aero road bikes. It can be confusing but it does ensure there's a bike for you…

Racing (road) bikes

As the name suggests, this road bike is all about speed. Its geometry's angled to send the rider into a sporty position. As such, the headtube will be steeper than an endurance bike, and will sport a short wheelbase and long reach to the handlebars for the all-important stretch. It'll also be stiffer for greater power transfer but at the sacrifice of comfort, while gear selection is more about generating power than cruising around the countryside.

Modern road bikes often have combined brake levers and gear changers (often called 'shifters'). The traditional drop handlebars allow the rider to assume a more efficient aerodynamic riding position.

Endurance (road) bikes

This is a relatively new addition to cycling's road line-up, featuring a more-relaxed geometry than a race bike, frames that are tuned to smooth out the ride and the potential to add wider tyres. It's all designed to make the ride more comfortable, and so are ideal for challenging events and long-distance riding. Endurance bikes also tend to have a longer wheelbase – the distance between respective wheel axles – which makes them more stable. In general, they come with a higher handlebar position than traditional road-racing bikes to reduce the strain on your neck and back. This geometry change gives a slightly less aerodynamic position but is far more comfortable on longer rides.

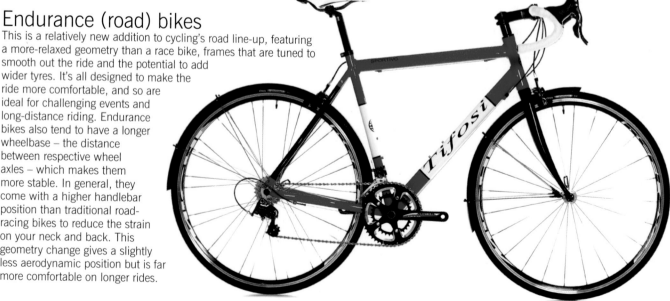

The traditional mountain bike often comes with front-fork suspension for a more comfortable off-road ride.

Downhill bikes feature further suspension for greater damping qualities.

Mountain bikes

Mountain Bikes encompass some of the most varied styles of bike available. Some are racey – designed to travel very fast over less challenging terrain while at the other end of the spectrum Downhill Mountain Bikes are designed to cope with incredibly steep gradients and huge obstacles, whilst being almost impossible to ride on the flat ground for any distance. Their tight geometry and high-volume tyres are designed to absorb nature's – and manmade – undulations. Many feature suspension in the front fork or within the frame itself.

Mountain bikes are commonly constructed from carbon, aluminium, steel and titanium; come with disc brakes as standard; and feature different wheel sizes depending on intended use. Historically mountain bikes featured wheels that measured 26in in diameter before 27.5in (650b) became the norm. Manufacturers have also experimented with larger wheel sizes like the 29-incher (same size as 700c road wheel), which rolled over obstacles more easily though weighed more. This has become the norm because of its ability to provide greater traction and speed.

In recent years, fat bikes have taken off. As the name suggests, these are mountain bikes that feature tyre widths of 3.8in or more and trace their origins back to Alaskan framebuilders, who realised those larger wheels provided more grip over snow. The idea caught on and it's spread to the masses. Then there are downhill mountain bikes. These are generally heavier and stronger than traditional MTBs because they're designed for steep, rough terrain that often features jumps, drops, rocks and other obstacles. Front and rear suspension will also feature travel that can reach 200m to cope with the severe terrain.

29ers, like this one from Specialized, provide greater traction and speed.

Fat bikes are essentially mountain bikes with very wide tyres. They were originally designed to ride in the snow.

Aero road bikes

Aero road bikes are one of the industry's most recent developments. They are designed to be extremely streamlined, making them able to carve through the air more efficiently than any other drop handle barred bike. And it achieves this streamlined aim by: adopting skinny or aero-shaped tubes instead of round versions, as well as a cut-away seat tube; using integrated brakes; and employing internal cable routing. Aero road bikes also tend to come complete with deep-rim wheels, which are more aerodynamic.

Aero road bikes, like Boardman's Air 9.8, carve through the air with streamlined efficiency.

Triathlon/TT bikes

Time-trial (TT) and triathlon bikes provided the inspiration for aero road bikes, featuring similar curvaceous designs for improved aerodynamics. The seat-tube angle is steeper to project the rider further forward, allowing the rider to adopt an extremely aerodynamic and efficient riding position. This more streamlined position is proven in wind-tunnels to be significantly more aerodynamic than a standard set-up. Aerobars and the bikes extreme aerodynamic geometry make this type of bike harder to handle so these bikes are more for non-drafting triathlons or time-trial races rather than mass events. TT bikes and triathlon bikes are very similar, though triathlon bikes often feature greater fuelling storage options like on the top tube. Note that the more aerodynamic a bike is the less comfortable it is making TT/Tri bikes uncomfortable over long distances.

Specialized's Shiv triathlon bike features an integrated hydration system that provides fuelling while remaining aerodynamic.

Cyclocross bikes

From a distance, cyclocross bikes look remarkably similar to road bikes, but edge closer and you'll discover some subtle but significant differences. The first is slightly wider and knobblier tyres, designed for increased grip and stability for off-road riding. There's also greater clearance between the tyre and frame, helping them cope with muddy conditions. Disc brakes near enough come as standard, these work better than calipers off-road. Gearing is also leg-friendly, aimed at spinning over the greater resistance of soil.

Cyclocross bikes might look like road bikes but subtle differences make them 'dirt friendly'.

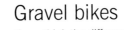

Gravel bikes have many of the attributes of cyclocross bikes but are better suited to longer rides.

Gravel bikes

If you think the difference between cyclocross and road bikes is subtle, then the difference between a cyclocross and gravel bike is a hair's breadth. The primary difference is that gravel bikes are less about racing and more for long days in the saddle over a mix of terrains. They feature eyelets for mudguards and racks for carrying luggage. A gravel bike's frame geometry is also slightly shallower for a more relaxed and comfortable ride. They have the capacity to fit wider tyres and a wide range of gears aimed at more leisurely, longer rides.

Fixed-gear bikes

A fixed-gear bike is simply one without a freewheel at the rear hub, which means no coasting. They arouse consternation and joy amongst the cycling community but, love them or loathe them, they do have their benefits. The first arises from the fact you'll freewheel on more traditional bikes an average 10–30% of every ride. With fixies that's not possible, so you make your nervous and muscular system work much harder; in fact, some say an hour on a fixie equates to two on a road bike. Because a fixie dispenses with gears, it's also easy to maintain. A single-speed bike is predominantly the same but you can freewheel. Many bikes in this genre feature a flip-flop hub where you can seamlessly change from a fixie to single-speed.

You can't freewheel on fixed-gear bikes, guaranteeing every ride is a tough workout.

Hybrid bikes

As the name suggests, these combine aspects of the traditional road bike and elements from the mountain bike to produce the ideal commuter or city bike. Most will feature 700c wheels with wider rims and 700 x 32 tyres, although some models use a 26in wheel with a narrow (1.9 inch, or less) tyre which usually has a slick or semi slick tread pattern.

At the lower end of the market you should expect a steel (or possibly aluminium) frame that comes with derailleur gears and V-type brakes. Mid-range models may feature cable disc brakes, a suspension fork and butted frame tubes. High-end models will often feature hub gears, hydraulic disc brakes and a quality suspension fork.

With their upright riding position, flat handlebars and the ability to negotiate potholes and kerbs, they are a perfect choice for a commuter bike. They also make ideal shopping or light touring bikes, as many have the necessary frame fixings to allow a rack and panniers to be easily fitted.

Touring bikes

In many ways touring bikes are heavy-duty racing bikes but with slacker frame angles and the addition of various fixing points on the frame to allow a rack and panniers to be fitted. Traditional touring bikes have drop handlebars, but many now feature mountain-bike-style flat or raised handlebars. Some modern touring bikes have adopted the 26in wheels of the mountain bike to provide a go-anywhere, all-terrain touring bike. For the serious world-tour cyclist, a custom steel frame will always be the first choice, as a steel frame can be repaired almost anywhere in the world.

This touring bike features a rear pannier rack, mudguards and a steel frame. Note also the 36-spoke wheels to provide plenty of support for the heavy load of the rider and all their touring luggage.

Folding bikes

Like e-bikes, folding-bike use is on the rise, their convenience and reasonable price point are an attraction for many. Of course, they're not as swift as their road-bike counterparts, 16 or 20 inch wheels are more about how many road bikes can you fold up and carry on the bus? That folding ability raises the question of weight. As you'll often be carrying the folder by hand, the lighter the better. Typically, though, this cranks up cost.

This folding bike from Bickerton rather impressively features gears, mudguards and even pannier racks.

E-bikes

Electric bikes – aka e-bikes – are becoming increasingly popular around the world. Take the Netherlands, for instance, where one in five bikes purchased now features an electric motor. The idea is pretty simple – a battery pack, often located on the downtube, feeds the motor that can kick in as and when you desire. You still need to pedal but have the option of taking it easy against a headwind or up a hill. They're perfect for commuters and come in all categories.

E-bikes (electric bikes) are growing in popularity, especially with commuters.

SIZING YOUR BIKE

Choosing the right size bike used to be a straightforward affair when all bikes had a simple triangular main frame and the top tube was more or less horizontal to the ground. Manufacturers based the frame size on the distance from the centre of the bottom-bracket spindle to the centre of the seat-post pinch bolt (or the top of the seat tube). The length of the top tube would increase in proportion to the length of the seat tube. Once you knew what size bike you required, it was easy (more or less) to switch from one manufacturer's bike to another and have no worries about the size being different.

The advent of the mountain bike, with its sloping top tube, and the compact road bike put paid to that simple equation. Add to this the arrival of the 'A-head' headset system (with its ability to easily swap stems) and super-long seat posts (up to 300mm), and getting the correct bike size became a confusing affair. Many manufacturers have abandoned frame sizes based on measurement and now simply list their bikes as 'small', 'medium' and 'large', and then suggest a recommended rider height for each size of frame.

For those that are based on frame size, see the table below. It shows frame sizes for mountain biking (MTB) and road (R). However, it's still best to seek out advice from your local bike shop, especially as many now have demonstrator bikes that can be loaned or hired for the day. The hire fee is normally refunded if you buy the bike. However, it would be impractical for bike shops to keep all models in all sizes as demo bikes, so don't expect your local shop to stock an XXL carbon fibre road bike!

FRAME SIZE (MTB)	FRAME SIZE (R)	INSIDE LEG
15in	38cm	24in–29in
16in	41cm	25in–30in
17in	43cm	26in–31in
18in	46cm	27in–32in
19in	49cm	28in–33in
20in	51cm	29in–34in
21in	54cm	30in–35in
22in	56cm	31in–36in
23in	59cm	32in–37in

TRIATHLON BIKE

Time trial (TT) and triathlon bikes are designed for speed. That's why they have an aerodynamic design, time-trial bars, aero wheels and a low front end. It's more important than ever to get the right size TT bike so that you're in the most aerodynamic riding position, and it's especially important if you're racing over long distances.

Rider height	Frame size
148cm-152cm	47cm-48cm
152cm-160cm	49cm-50cm
160cm-168cm	51cm-53cm
168cm-175cm	54cm-55cm
175cm-183cm	56cm-58cm
183cm-191cm	58cm-60cm
191cm-198cm	61cm-63cm

HYBRID BIKES

Hybrids are typically used for commuting or leisure riding. They often incorporate mountain-bike styling but with smoother and narrower tyres. Or they look like a road bike but with flat handlebars. When choosing your hybrid bike, it's best to consider whether you'll be riding mainly on- or off-road.

Rider height	Frame sizes
148cm-158cm	13in-14in
158cm-168cm	15in-16in
168cm-178cm	17in-18in
178cm-185cm	19in-20in
185cm-193cm	21in-22in
193cm-198cm	23in-24in

Women's bikes

Women's bicycles used to be solely characterised by a lack of top tube and curvaceous downtube. These elegant Dutch-style step-through bikes remain popular but now all forms of bike feature women-specific touches designed for the female form.

Road bikes designed for female riders now carry the moniker 'WSD', meaning women-specific design. Where once lazy manufacturers would simply apply a coating of pink paint, WSD signifies bikes that tend to feature shorter top tubes, which compensate for the smaller upper body of women, and longer seat tubes to cater for women's proportionally longer legs. Crank length might also be shorter and, in the world of mountain biking, a bike may well feature custom-tuned suspension forks. You'll also find that smaller women's road bikes might feature 650c wheels rather than the standard 700c wheels seen on the majority of road bikes.

However, it pays to examine the manufacturers' catalogues in detail, as their women-specific bikes may only differ from the men's versions by a few millimetres. Or indeed, it may be exactly the same frame as the men's version but with a shorter stem, a female-specific saddle and shorter cranks. And, of course, it will be painted in an appropriate 'female' colour. You may well be paying a premium price for these small changes, and it can often work out significantly cheaper to adapt a men's frame (by swapping stems and saddle, for instance) rather than paying the premium price for the WSD bike.

The classic step-through frame is still a viable option for many women. Continental-style (or 'Dutch') bikes often feature fully enclosed chains, dynamo-powered lights, integral locks, hub gears and coaster brakes. Whilst not suitable for long trips, they're perfect for running errands or an evening out in town.

Perhaps the biggest issue for many women is getting a comfortable saddle. In recent years, many women-specific saddles have begun to appear on the market. They all tend to be broader at the rear and shorter overall and many are gel-filled to give a soft and comfortable ride – in theory. However, soft doesn't always mean comfortable. Serious cyclists tend to prefer a firmer saddle. One option is to fit a gel-filled saddle cover to start – assuming you have a firm women's saddle fitted – and then try riding without it on short trips. Either way, getting a comfortable saddle will always boil down to personal preference.

A good women's bike, like this model from Liv, features women-specific geometry and components.

This small-framed women's racing bike is suitable for the serious cyclist, but unless your workplace has changing facilities it's not suitable for commuting.

This classic 'retro' women's bike harks back to times gone by.

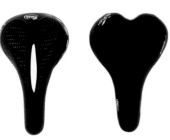

Just as for men, a wide variety of saddles are available for women. The saddle on the left is more suited to racing and serious cycling, whilst the one on the right is much more of a recreational saddle. As mentioned, saddle choice is very much a matter of personal preference.

Adjusting a bike to suit

1 A layback seatpost can create more 'room' for a rider but will also change the riding and pedalling position.

2 Quality brake levers will allow adjustment for reach.

3 Adjustable stems allow you to 'tweak' your riding position. Note that these stems are not suitable for off-road use.

Setting your riding position

Assuming you've purchased a bike of the right size, next you'll need to make some minor adjustments to the riding position. It's easy to spot cyclists who haven't got this right because they're either on the wrong size of bike or their riding position needs adjusting. You'll see riders with their hips rocking on too large a bike (or with the saddle too high), and you'll see riders whose knees appear to be hitting their chins where the bike is too small or seatpost too low.

Beyond the discomfort factor, incorrect bike fit can result in injuries, especially around the knee area. So how do you achieve the perfect bike fit? Search online and you'll discover a plethora of fitting options but, if you can afford it, the ideal is a professional fitting.

A respected bike-fitter will take into account your individual needs, anatomy and cycling aims. For instance, if you're looking to mimic a streamlined Chris Froome in a time-trial, your position will be markedly different than if you've just bought your first step-through bike in search of an upright and comfortable position. The professional will assess your flexibility and strength, measure your limbs and even prescribe orthotics if needed. Usually it'll set you back around £100 or more but it's money well spent.

Failing that, as long as you're meticulous with the process, a DIY bike-fit is fine. We recommend the 109% method. This scientifically supported formula has shown that the saddle height for generating the most efficient pedal stroke is 109% of your inside leg measurement. Simply measure the length of your inside leg from the floor to the crotch. Do this standing without shoes on. Multiply this length by 109%, and this will give you the length from the top of the saddle to the extended pedal at the bottom of the stroke. So if your inside seam is 81cm, height between pedal and saddle should be around 88cm.

You then move onto the fore-and-aft position of the saddle. This is the horizontal position. Initially set the saddle level and the seatpost clamp in the centre of the saddle rails. Sit on the bike and rotate the cranks to the horizontal position. Using a plumb line, check to see if your knee is directly above the centre of the pedal. If not, move the saddle forwards or backwards as necessary.

With the saddle correctly adjusted, move onto the position of the handlebars. This will depend greatly on the type of bike you ride and the type of riding you intend to do. If the bike is fitted with an A-head system then the height of the cycle's handlebars can be adjusted by adding or removing spacers from underneath the stem. If the cycle is fitted with a more traditional 'quill' stem then the central bolt must be loosened before the height of the stem and subsequently, handlebars, can be changed. It is *vital* that the stem is correctly done up again before the bike is ridden. You *must* be able to brake and steer properly for a bike to be safe to ride. If in any doubt consult a qualified mechanic. For a leisurely ride to the local shop, a near upright position will be fine; for aggressive off-road riding, you'll need to be leaning forward so that some of your weight is over the front wheel. This aids traction and steering control.

For the classic road bike with drop handlebars, riding position is much lower and far more aerodynamic when your hands are on the drop section of the bars. In this position you're in a head-down posture. However, be warned: even on a racing bike you'll be spending most of your time on the top flat section of the bars, with your hands just behind or resting on the brake-lever hoods. In this position your back will be at around 45° to the ground. Again this all depends on your personal preferences. Many road-riders prefer to be slightly more upright when cruising, but will push themselves further back in the saddle when on the 'drops'.

For a lot of riders the setting of the riding position will require further small adjustments of the bars, stem and saddle rather than adherence to some hard and fast rule. If it feels right and suits your particular type of riding then all will be fine.

With the ball of the foot on the pedal, the lower leg will be slightly bent. The rider in the picture is using clip-in pedals and shoes with cleats. These ensure that the ball of the foot is always correctly positioned.

An improvised plumb line can help with establishing the fore/aft position of the saddle.

Children's bikes

Bikes for children tend to be based on wheel size rather than frame size. The table below can be used as a rough guide to bike size based on age. The biggest mistake made by parents when buying their child's first bike is to buy one that's too big with the hope that 'they'll grow into it'. Nothing puts a child off riding more than an oversized bike. Yes, they will no doubt grow to achieve a perfect fit, but by then they'll have become so frustrated by the experience that they may never want to ride a bike again.

Things start with balance bikes – see page 17 for more. You then have bikes with 14in and 16in wheels that are often built rather parochially, with cheap components fitted, but they're functional and will last a reasonable length of time with some basic maintenance. Pay particular attention to the often flimsy caliper-type brakes on such bikes, though, as small hands often lack the strength to operate them if the cables are worn or the pivot points are poorly adjusted and lacking lubrication.

The larger the wheel size, the more the bike becomes a scaled-down adults' bike. 20in-wheeled BMX ('bicycle moto-cross') bikes are some of the most robust available and suit children from around nine years old to adult. Their simple single-speed set-up also means maintenance is straightforward and uncomplicated. 24in-wheeled bikes are also suitable for small adults. Quality components are often fitted to the more expensive of these. If the bike is likely to become a hand-me-down to the child's siblings, then consider paying the extra for a top-of-the-range model.

Try to avoid buying children a fashion or trendy bike. In the larger wheel sizes, a simple old-fashioned triangular-framed bike is still the best option. Also, unless you're buying at the top of the range, avoid bikes with suspension components, as these are often crude and heavy.

A balance bike acclimatises your child to the feeling of riding on two wheels.

WHEEL SIZE	AGE
14in	2 to 5
16in	5 to 7
20in	7 to 9
24in	9 to 11
26in	11 plus

24inch wheels

Often fitted with derailleur gears, sealed bearings and alloy rims, these are very much scaled-down adult bikes. With a sloping top tube and a long seat post these will suit a wide range of heights. Top-of-the-range models will feature 'A-head' type headsets, V brakes and indexed derailleur gears.

BMX bikes

This is a 16in BMX – most feature 20in wheels. With its large-volume tyres and 36-spoke wheels (or 48 on heavy-duty models), these bikes will take a tremendous amount of use and abuse. They're a great choice for learning off-road skills, such as jumping, but no use for long-distance rides.

14inch wheels

Often supplied with stabilisers, these are the first bike for many children. Remove the stabilisers as soon as the child grows in confidence.

16inch wheels

These may be supplied with stabilisers, but these will only be needed by children who lack confidence. Some may have six- or seven-speed gear systems fitted. Suitable for short family excursions.

20inch wheels

Suitable for boys and girls from the age of about seven onwards, they can either be single-speed or have derailleur gears.

Teaching children to ride

For years, many of us followed the cycling learning pathway of: trike, bike with stabilisers followed by bike with stabilisers removed. That route to cycling proficiency still stands, of course, and we'll come onto that shortly. But in recent years, balance bikes have become an increasingly employed tool to teach cycling skills.

A balance bike is simply a bike without pedals, gears or chain, and children push themselves along with their feet. This means that instead of trying to learn to pedal, balance and brake all in one go, they already have the balance aspect mastered for when they are ready for a pedal bike.

There are many types of balance bikes out there, but the primary consideration is the size of the frame – too big and a small toddler will struggle; too small and it's not going to work for an older child. You should also consider how adjustable the seat is.

Still, even with the use of balance bikes, the leap to pedalling without stabilisers can be too great. That's where a kids' bike with stabilisers comes in. This instils confidence and allows the child to understand steering and braking without having to worry about balancing as well. When to remove the stabilisers can be a difficult call. As soon as they're accelerating and riding short distances without one of the stabilisers on the ground might be the right time to remove them.

The best place to learn without stabilisers is on a gentle grassy slope. The slope should be steep enough to allow the bike to freewheel without any pedal input. In an ideal world the slope will have a slight rise at the bottom to scrub off any speed the rider may have gained. Have the child stand with their feet firmly on the ground (lower the saddle if necessary), and then have them lift up their feet and let the bike roll down the hill. It's best to follow them down with one hand just under (but not touching) the saddle. Grab the saddle and support the bike if a tumble is imminent. As they grow in confidence, encourage them to lift their feet on to the pedals. For the final stage, get them to pedal as well.

Once they're confident, the saddle can be raised to the correct position. It's then time to introduce them to some simple bike-control exercises. Have them stop on a line and get them to weave in and out of a series of cones. Move the cones closer together as their bike-handling skills improve. When you're happy with their bike control, it's time to introduce them to the highway. Start on a quiet residential street and always cycle behind them – not too close, but within hailing distance.

Finally, all novice riders should have some formal training. This will often be offered at school, but if in doubt contact Bikeability (www.dft. gov.uk/bikeability) for details of training schemes in your area.

Always encourage children to wear a helmet at all times, especially when they're learning to ride.

CHAPTER

ROUTINE MAINTENANCE AND REPAIRS

Name that part

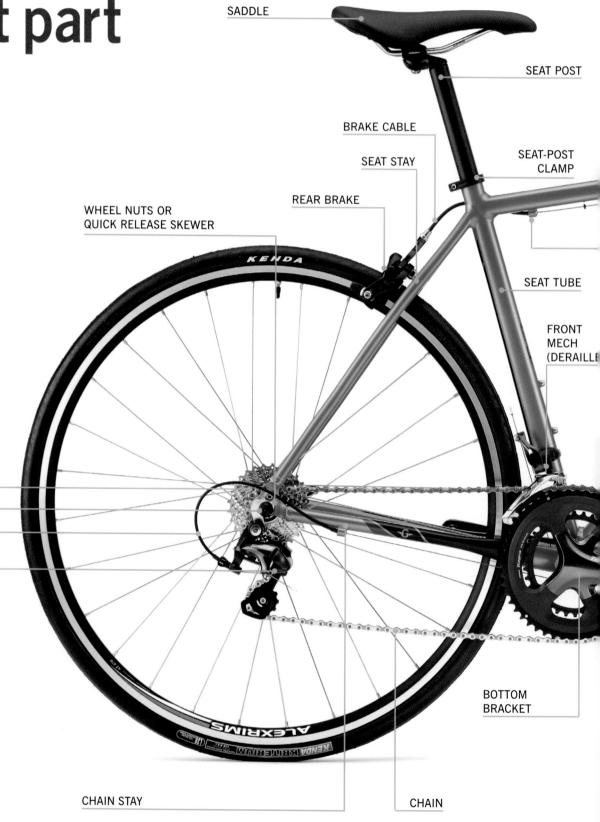

SADDLE

SEAT POST

BRAKE CABLE

SEAT-POST CLAMP

SEAT STAY

REAR BRAKE

WHEEL NUTS OR QUICK RELEASE SKEWER

SEAT TUBE

FRONT MECH (DERAILLE

MULTIPLE FREEWHEEL OR CASSETTE

REAR DROP OUT

GEAR CABLE

REAR MECH (DERAILLEUR)

BOTTOM BRACKET

CHAIN STAY

CHAIN

BRAKE LEVER/
GEAR SHIFTERS

STEM

HANDLEBARS

HEADSET SPACERS

HEADSET

TOP TUBE

HEAD TUBE

FRONT BRAKE

TYRE VALVE

CABLE STOP

FRONT WHEEL

DOWN TUBE

SPOKE

TYRE

FORKS

HUB

RIM

CHAINRINGS

CRANKS

SPOKE NIPPLE

WHEEL NUTS OR
QUICK RELEASE SKEWERS

FORK DROPOUT

ALTERNATIVE SADDLES

WOMEN'S SADDLE
Wider at the rear to suit the female anatomy.

SPRUNG SADDLE
The traditional saddle is good for touring.

'I' BEAM
A single, much wider rail located centrally on the underside of the saddle.

ALTERNATIVE HANDLEBARS

  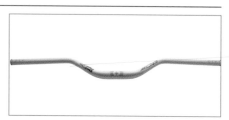

DROP HANDLEBARS
These are generally used on road, touring and cyclo-cross (CX) bikes.

FLAT HANDLEBARS
For kids' bikes, commuter bikes and mountain bikes.

RISER BARS
Lots of styles and types available. Used on mountain bikes and commuter bikes.

ALTERNATIVE GEARING SYSTEMS

HUB GEARS
Proving popular once again due to their low maintenance.

SINGLE-SPEED GEAR
Single-speed is commonly used on kids' bikes and BMX bikes. A cult following has developed for single-speed amongst mountain bikers and commuters in recent years.

ALTERNATIVE TYRES

26IN SLICK
High aspect ratio tyres with little or no tread for on-road use.

700C ROAD TYRE
For road bikes, commuters and tourers.

Tools

A good selection of tools will always be required. Every cyclist should start with a basic toolkit for on-the-road (or trail) repairs. This should be carried at all times and contain enough tools to enable most basic repairs to be carried out. Many cyclists add a spare inner tube to their basic on-the-road kit and pack it all into a small seat-post-mounted bag. Add a frame-mounted pump, and you'll have all the basic tools you'll need when out riding.

A basic home toolkit will add some general hand tools and a few specialist bicycle tools. A bike-cleaning kit will be needed, as well as a selection of oils and lubricants. Some means of supporting the bike while carrying out repairs will also be useful.

An advanced home toolkit will contain many specialist and specific hand tools. A proper bike repair stand can be added, and for the serious home mechanic a wheel-truing stand will be essential.

Most of the tools shown here are in addition to the standard tools that many riders will already have.

The minimalist rider's toolkit

This is perhaps the minimum toolkit you can get away with. The multi-tool covers most eventualities. You will, of course, need to add a pump or CO_2 canisters.

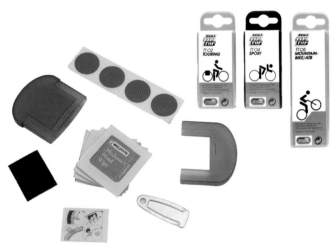

PUNCTURE KIT
Essential – never leave home without one. Self-adhesive patches are a quick and reliable repair, but may cyclists prefer the traditional puncture repair kit.

TYRE LEVERS
Use with caution, but essential on tight-fitting tyres.

MULTI-TOOL
A vast choice is now available. Many incorporate a chain tool.

SPARE INNER TUBE
Not essential, but easier than repairing a puncture on a cold, wet day.

CHAIN TOOL
Not required if your multi-tool incorporates one.

CONNECTING CHAIN LINK
Not essential, but useful if you snap your chain.

Universal tools

Pliers – Combination pliers have many uses. Ideal for pulling brake and derailleur inner cables tight.

Adjustable spanner – A good option if you encounter worn or obscure-sized nuts or bolts. Very useful for tightening the lock nuts on traditional threaded steerer forks.

Combination metric spanners – A range from 8mm to 19mm will be useful.

Screwdrivers – A small cross-head or slotted screwdriver will be required for adjusting derailleurs and brakes.

Mallet – Nylon or rubber (or hide/copper) Essential for removing some components without causing damage.

Socket set ($^3/_8$in drive) – Whilst not essential, these do speed up many tasks. BMX footpegs and some suspension forks can only be removed with a socket.

Scriber – Great for opening the ends of cables after they've been cut. Also very useful for picking the dirt out of hex and torx key fittings.

Basic home toolkit

HEADSET SPANNERS
Often used in conjunction with an adjustable spanner, and essential for adjusting play in traditional threaded headset bearings.

CABLE CUTTERS
Of all the specialist bike tools available, cable cutters are perhaps the most frequently used. It will be well worth spending extra money on a high-quality pair that will last you for many years.

CONE SPANNERS
An essential specialist tool. This set of five will cover most requirements.

CHAIN CHECKER
The simplest and most effective way of checking a chain for wear. Several versions are available.

TORX KEY SET
In recent years torx fittings have started to appear on bicycles. At the moment they're mostly confined to chainring bolts and brake rotor mounting bolts. A folding key set is perfectly adequate.

HEX KEY SET
Most mid- to high-end bikes won't have any traditional nuts and bolts fitted. They all have hex bolt fittings (often referred to as Allen bolts), so a wide variety of hex keys including a folding set and a ball end set will be required.

CHAIN BREAKER
This heavy-duty chain breaker will provide many years of sterling service.

CRANK REMOVER
Essential for removing the crank arms from square taper and the various designs of splined cranks. The one designed for splined cranks has a slightly larger head, although with a little ingenuity the square taper one can be used.

CASSETTE/REAR SPROCKET REMOVAL TOOLS
Before the arrival of the freehub and cassette most rear sprockets were screwed to the hub. Each manufacturer produced their own unique sprocket removal tool.

CHAIN WHIP
A chain whip tool will be required to hold the cassette in position while the lockring is removed. A simple tool that's very easy to fabricate out of a piece of scrap metal bar and some lengths of chain.

PEDAL SPANNER
It's possible to remove some pedals with a standard 15mm open-ended spanner. However, most standard spanners are too broad to fit into the gap between the crank on the pedal, in which case a special narrow pedal spanner will be required. Some modern pedals don't have the flat side and can only be removed with a hex key from the rear of the crank arm.

SPOKE KEYS
Unfortunately there's no standard size for spoke nipples, so a selection of spoke keys will be required. Again, buy the one for the bike you will be working on then build up your collection, buying a new one each time you need one'

BOTTOM BRACKET TOOLS
A wide selection will be required to deal with the various types of bottom bracket. Buy the type of Bottom Bracket tool for the bike(s) you will be working on, then build up your selection as you go.

Advanced home toolkit

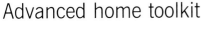

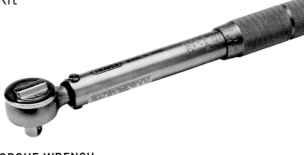

CHAINRING TOOL
Whilst a broad screwdriver can often be used, there's no substitute for the correct tool, especially given the low cost of a chainring spanner.

TORQUE WRENCH
This 10 to 80Nm, $^3/_8$in drive torque wrench from Draper is ideal. If you're lucky enough to have carbon fibre components on your bicycle, then this preset (at 5Nm) T-handled torque wrench is essential, as many carbon fibre components must be tightened correctly.

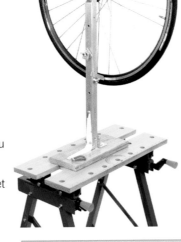

DISHING TOOL
Used to check that the rim lies over the centreline of the hub. If you've fabricated a wheel truing jig, then flipping the wheel over in it produces the same result.

HEADSET PRESS
This is the professional tool. Headset presses can be expensive but well worth it if you are putting headsets in to bikes several times during the year. Most modern bikes have headset bearings that press directly into the frame – for these a headset press is not required .

WHEEL TRUING JIG
Professional wheel truing jigs are available, but are relatively expensive. We fabricated this simple jig from a length of box-section aluminium mounted in a folding workbench.

CROWN RACE PULLER
A useful tool if you replace headsets often. Many headsets these days are supplied with a split crown race that's easily removable from the fork steerer. A crown race puller isn't required with a split crown race headset.

VERNIER GAUGE
A useful addition to the home mechanic toolbox. Great for measuring seat post diameters, chain widths and head tube diameters.

SPOKE RULER
A must-have if you get serious about wheel building or spoke replacement.

LARGE SOCKET
Specific (½in drive) sockets may be required to service suspension forks, which often have a very shallow spring or damper retaining nut fitted. A thin rag or paper towel placed over the nut will help avoid a slip and any consequent damage.

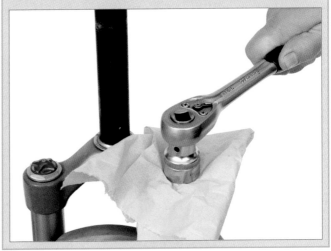

How to use tools

Learning how to use tools correctly will minimise the chances of personal injury and damage to tools and equipment. Where possible always loosen fixings by pulling towards yourself and not pushing away. If you're working on standard six-sided (hexagonal) nuts and bolts, always choose a ring spanner in preference to an open-ended spanner. Ring spanners are less likely to slip, and good-quality ones will apply an even force to all six sides of the fixing.

When working on 'hex'-type bolts – often called Allen bolts – use the best-quality hex keys you can afford. Use a small pick to remove any debris from the fixing if necessary and flush it with a suitable cleaner to ensure the key bottoms out in the bolt. This is especially important on hex bolts with shallow heads.

'Torx'-type bolts are also starting to make an appearance on bicycles, and often have a shallower head than the equivalent hex bolt, so the same considerations with regard to cleaning apply, but more so.

How tight is tight enough? The simple answer would be to use a torque wrench that allows torque setting to be preset at all times, but if you're out riding you'll just have to trust your own judgement and experience. If you're unsure if a component is tightened sufficiently, have someone more experienced check it over. Be careful, because most beginners tend to over tighten fixings which can lead to serious damage to components. Also remember that safety-critical components should always be tightened correctly with a torque wrench.

If you have a fixing that seems to constantly loosen itself over time then consider replacing the nut or bolt. Alternatively use a self-locking nut ('nylok' has become the generic name for such nuts), spring washer or a suitable thread-locking compound.

When dealing with brake and gear cables, a quality pair of cable cutters is essential. This will often be the home mechanic's first specialist tool purchase. They'll be used frequently, so buy the best you can afford. When cutting a spiral-wound outer cable, it may be necessary to file the end flat to remove any sharp edges. When cutting newer-style gear cables, the end of the cable and liner tend to become flattened, so use a small pick to open them out. An engineer's scribing tool or old bicycle spoke are ideal for this.

Where possible start off threaded nuts and bolts by hand to make sure you are not cross threading them.

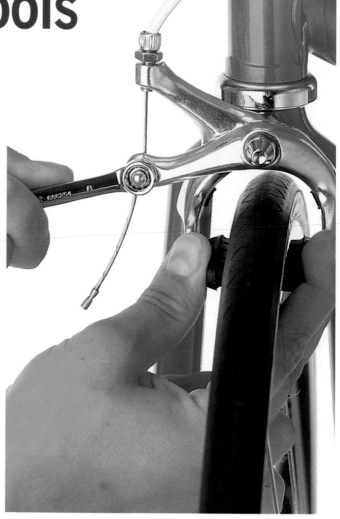

1 If possible, always use a ring spanner in preference to an open-ended spanner. They apply an equal force on all the flats of the bolt and are less likely to slip.

2 Consider covering the chainrings with a protective cloth or shifting the chain into the outer chain ring when removing or installing pedals. A slip here can be painful.

3 A set of long-reach T-handled Allen keys make life easier, but don't over-tighten the fixing when using the short end of the key.

4 If you only have a standard set of Allen keys and need to access a deeply recessed fitting, it's possible to fit a short length of tube over the short end of the key for extra leverage.

5 The three-legged hex key is a mechanic's favourite as it contains the most common key sizes found on bikes. A great tool for a quick check of most of the fixings on a bike.

6 Use a small pick to clean debris from hex and torx fixings. This ensures the key bottoms out in the fixing.

7 A snug-fitting cross-head or flat-blade screwdriver is essential for adjusting the high- and low-stop screws on derailleur-equipped bikes.

8 Cut the inner cable cleanly, leaving about 50mm below the clamp bolt. If the cable starts to unravel, twist it carefully in the direction of the spiral winding.

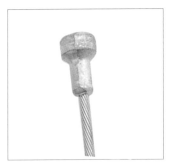

9 Fit a cable end fitting as soon as the cable has been cut. If you have no fittings, a dab of superglue is a good temporary solution.

10 Both brake and gear cables should have ferrules fitted. Metal ones are fitted to brake cables and plastic ones to gear cables. It's sometimes possible to reuse the old fittings, but check them carefully first.

11 Gear cables are thinner than brake cables. The latter tend to be spiral-wound while gear cables tend to have their inner strands running parallel.

12 Gear cable end fittings are universal, whilst those of brake cables vary. Note that brake cables often have fittings on both ends. Cut off the redundant one.

Monthly checks

There are some bike checks that must be undertaken each and every month. These are especially important if you're racking up hundreds of miles each month and doing so over a tough winter. When it comes to checking for wear, none of these jobs require any specialist tools.

1 Check the rim braking surface for wear and damage. This rim has seen better days.

2 Check the security of the rotor.

3 Check for loose or damaged spokes.

4 Check the brake cables for damage and wear to the outer cable. This inner cable requires immediate replacement.

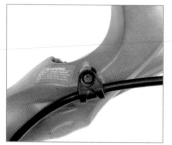

5 On bikes with hydraulic brakes check the hose for chafing. Pay particular attention to anywhere that the hose is clamped to the frame or the forks.

6 Pull on the front brake and rock the bike back and forth to check for play in the headset bearings.

7 Grasp the saddle and check that it's secure.

8 Check the tyre sidewalls for damage. This tyre needs replacing.

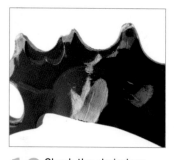

9 Grab the cranks and push them in and out to check for play.

10 Check the chainrings for worn and damaged teeth. This chainring has a broken tooth.

11 Check the rear sprockets or cassette for wear and damage. Also check the chain for wear and damage. A broken chain can be dangerous, painful and expensive.

12 Check the rear derailleur for alignment and worn jockey wheels. This jockey wheel requires immediate replacement.

13 On bikes with front suspension, check for oil leaks and wear. Oil is starting to leak from this front suspension fork.

14 On full suspension bikes check for wear in the pivots.

Pre-ride quick check

A quick check-over before any ride is always a good idea. Concentrate on the safety-critical items before looking at the drivetrain and 'comfort' items. After all, a loose bottle cage, whilst inconvenient, won't be a disaster, but a loose wheel will!

None of the checks (apart from tyre pressures) require any tools, but it may be worth having a multi-tool in your pocket in case any adjustment or tightening is required.

1 Check the security of the wheels in the dropouts.

2 Grasp the front wheel at the rim and rock it from side to side to check for play in the bearings. Lift the wheel and spin it. Listen for the noise of worn or damaged bearings.

3 Do the same for the rear wheel. A small amount of play is acceptable.

4 Check the brake pads for wear and tear.

5 Check that the pads meet the rim correctly.

6 On bikes with disc brakes check the pads for wear.

7 Check the security of the handlebars. Hold the wheel and try to turn the bars.

8 Check the tyre treads for wear and foreign objects.

9 Check the tyre pressures.

Wheel removal

Most bikes will have some method of releasing the brake caliper to allow the tyre to pass the brake blocks. See Chapter 3 for full instructions on releasing the common type of brake caliper. On bikes fitted with derailleur gears, select the highest gear – the smallest sprocket on the rear wheel. On bikes with hub gears, release the selector cable, as described in Chapter 4.

Turn the bike upside down or mount it in a work stand if you have one. On bikes fitted with quick-release (QR) wheels, open the quick release and, at the rear, pull the wheel free. This is easily achieved on mountain bikes and newer road bikes with vertical dropouts (the slots in the frame where the wheel mounts). On bikes with horizontal or near-horizontal dropouts, removing the wheel can be more of a fiddle. On single-speed and hub-geared bikes you'll need to push the wheel forward to enable the chain to be unhooked. On derailleur bikes the rear block just needs to clear the chain.

At the front you'll need to release the QR and undo the nut several revolutions to clear the safety tabs on the dropouts. On mountain bikes fitted with bolt-through axles, you'll need to release the QR and then undo the axle.

Bikes fitted with hub nuts will require two correct-sized spanners. Release the axle nuts and note the position of any washers fitted. There's normally one washer on the outboard side of the dropout, unless flanged hub nuts are fitted. There may also be a washer fitted to the inside.

Refitting is straightforward on bikes with vertical dropouts, as the wheel is automatically centred in the frame. On bikes with traditional semi-horizontal dropouts, the wheel must be aligned correctly. Pull the wheel back and, by sighting towards the bottom bracket, ensuring it's central in the frame.

On single-speed and hub-gear bikes you'll have to align the wheel in the frame and tension the chain at the same time. This can be difficult and time-consuming, especially if you have a bolt-in rear wheel.

Bolt-in wheels

1 First, drop the chain into the highest gear, then undo both wheel nuts three or four turns. Proper wheel nuts have a built-in toothed washer to grip the frame – change to this type if your bike only has plain nuts with a separate washer.

2 Pull the rear mech (derailleur) backwards so that the chain cage pivots right out of the way. This will allow the wheel to slide forward out of the dropouts, though it will be tight. Give it a hefty push with your free hand towards the bottom bracket and seat tube if it sticks.

3 As the wheel drops out of the frame, it will bring the chain with it. Let the rear mech return to its normal position and try to lift the wheel away. If it won't come you'll have to lift the chain out of the sprockets with your fingers.

4 When you're ready to refit the wheel, pivot the rear mech backwards again and engage the top sprocket with the top run of the chain. Lift the wheel so that the sprockets pass over the rear mech, bringing the chain with them.

5 Quickly check to see if the rim is centred and lift the axle into the frame. Pull the wheel back to the middle of the drop out, clear of the rear mech, then do the nuts up finger-tight. Check the rim is centred before tightening them.

6 On single-speed bikes, push the wheel forward to slacken the chain and then unhook it from the chainring. Pull the wheel backwards and unhook the chain from the sprocket.

Quick-release wheels

1 Loosening a quick release is a finger and thumb operation. Just hook your thumb round the lever and pull hard. As soon as you've overcome the initial locking action, the lever will swing back the rest of the way quite freely.

2 Hold the thumb nut with one hand and give the lever a couple of turns with the other to release the wheel.

3 When refitting the wheel, you may find that you have to spread the forks a little to fit the axle between them. If necessary you must tighten up the thumb nut so that the quick release almost bites before you operate the lever.

4 The initial movement of the quick-release lever requires little pressure. By the time it passes halfway it should need more force, and the final locking stage should take quite a lot. If it doesn't, it's not tight. Always aim to have the QR lever pointing to the rear of the bike.

RockShox thru-axle

1 When closed, the lever should be upright and run parallel to the fork. Pull down and simply rotate the lever anti-clockwise to remove the axle. The wheel will slot off.

2 Each frame and fork manufacturer's axle holes differ ever so slightly. With RockShox, the thru-axle comes with 12 combinations of torque setting.

3 Press the end of the thru-axle and rotate to access one of the combinations.

4 At the right torque the Thru axle lever will leave a slight impression in your hand when done up. Too tight and the device will break. Too loose and it won't hold the wheel.

Fox thru-axle

1 Like the RockShox, pull the lever towards you and rotate anti-clockwise to remove wheel.

2 When refitting the axle, you may have to undo the grub screw with a 2.5mm Allen key. Remove the nut and rotate until you find the perfect axle fit.

3 Again like the RockShox, the perfect fit leaves a small indent of the lever in your hand and the lever running parallel to the front fork.

BMX wheels

If you have a BMX bike with footpegs fitted at the front or rear, you'll need a socket and extension bar to access the wheel bolts.

Tyre and wheel care

Turn the bike upside down and give the front wheel a good spin. It should run smoothly with little noise. If it slows quickly or is noisy, the chances are you have a problem with the bearings – see Chapter 6. Do the same for the rear wheel, but don't expect it to run as smoothly due to the drag from the freewheel. Bikes with disc brakes will often exhibit noise due to the brake pads rubbing on the disc, especially sintered pads.

Next, grasp each tyre and check for play in the hub bearings by rocking the wheel in the frame (or forks) from side to side. A slight amount of play is fine on wheels with standard loose-bearing hubs, but not on bikes fitted with sealed bearings.

Next, slowly turn the wheel with your thumb gently resting against the rim. Eyeball the rim as it rotates past your thumb. A buckled rim will be obvious, but don't be confused by a bulge in the tyre sidewall. If you're unsure, remove the tyre (as described in the next section), refit the wheel to the bike and try again.

If the wheel is running out of true, check the spokes next. Start at the valve and check for broken and loose spokes. Any loose spokes should be tightened and the wheel trued. This procedure is explained in Chapter 6.

Again, working from the valve, inspect the rim for cracks and damage. Carefully inspect the braking surface for wear. Over time this will become concaved as the brake pads wear down the rim. Press firmly on any suspect areas of wear. A heavily worn surface will deflect under moderate pressure, but a full check can only be done with the tyre and tube removed. If necessary use a nylon scouring pad (Scotch-Brite) to clean the braking surface and remove any embedded grit particles.

Finally, inspect the tyre for nicks and cuts. Remove any flints and stones. Pay particular attention to the sidewall, especially on 700c road tyres as these tend to degrade rather than wear out. You may need to deflate the tyre to inspect it, if the sidewall seems to be perished or damaged.

Tyre and wheel check

1 With the wheel off the ground, give it a quick spin and watch the rim as it passes the brake blocks. On bikes with disc brakes, grasp the fork or frame and use your thumb as a guide. A badly buckled and out-of-true wheel will be easy to spot.

2 If the tyre isn't running straight, deflate it and refit it, making sure the beads fit into the well properly. Then, whether it's buckled or not, stretch each pair of spokes with your finger and thumb to see if they're correctly tensioned.

3 Go round the tyre with a small screwdriver, prising out any flints stuck in the tread. Look out for deep cuts, whether or not there's a flint embedded in them, and consider fitting a new tyre if there's any serious damage.

4 The tyre wall should be evenly coloured, with an unbroken coat of rubber all the way from the rim to the tread. If the fabric is showing or there are any cuts or splits, deflate the tyre so you can see how bad the damage is.

5 Round off the wheel check by turning the axle with your fingers. It should feel smooth, but if it feels tight or gritty, strip and re-grease it.

6 A nylon scouring pad is ideal for removing grit and dirt particles from the rim braking surface.

Inflating tyres

1 On Presta valves you must remove the dust cap and undo the knurled nut. Unseat the valve by pressing it with a finger (on an inflated tyre you'll hear the air escape) before fitting the pump.

2 Schrader valves are common on 26in-wheeled bikes. This is the standard valve used on all car tyres and, if you have a car foot pump, it can be used to inflate these tubes. Don't be tempted to use a high-pressure garage air line to inflate Schrader tubes, though – this is a dangerous practice.

3 Most pumps just push on to the valve, but the air will escape if you push the adaptor on too far. If you're having trouble, check that the adaptor is square on to the valve and steady your hand with a finger round the valve or a spoke.

4 Pump up the tyre until firm and then roll the wheel on the floor to settle the bead into position. Check that the bead is seated correctly and then fully inflate the tyre. See the appendix for a table of suggested tyre pressures.

5 When you've fully inflated a tyre with a Presta or Schrader valve, check that the valve is at right angles to the rim. On Presta (and some Schrader) tubes check that the securing ring is finger-tight. Don't over-tighten it as that might cause a puncture. Refit the dust cap.

Pumps

1 A track pump makes light work of pumping up tyres. An essential tool if you have a fleet of bikes to maintain.

2 Most track pumps have a dual head for both Presta and Schrader valves.

3 Mini-pumps are often dual action – they pump on both strokes. On road bikes a traditional frame-fitting pump is hard to beat.

Replacing tyres

When the time comes to replace your tyres, you'll be faced with a bewildering choice in the popular 26in, 29in and 700c market. Tyre choice is also good for 20in BMX bikes but limited for smaller children's bikes.

Bikes that see only occasional use in the summer months don't need state-of-the-art, Kevlar-beaded, race-proven exotic tyres. Tyres on these bikes will require replacement mostly because they've perished. A tyre from the budget end of the market will be suitable here.

For riders with bikes that have moderate to extreme use it's always worth purchasing a quality tyre. These will often have some puncture resistance in the form of a Kevlar (or similar) cloth woven into their fabric. They may even have different rubber compounds for different road or trail conditions. For road riding, most tyres will be smooth with little or no visible tread pattern. Tyres for commuter bikes often feature a central smooth section and a distinct tread pattern at the edges. This gives a lower rolling resistance when travelling in a straight line and additional grip when cornering.

The choice for mountain bikes is vast, from smooth, 'slick' road-style tyres right through to mud tyres with large, wide-spaced rubber spikes.

When fitting a new tyre, it's always a good idea to fit a new inner tube. Inner tubes are often sized to fit the tyre, so check that you buy one that's compatible with the tyre you're using.

Where possible, try to fit the new tyre without the use of tyre levers. On some rim and tyre combinations this is very easy; on others you may struggle. Some combinations will always require a tyre lever to flip the last section of bead over the rim. Occasionally you'll encounter a rim-and-tyre combination that just won't fit. This is often due to variations in the manufacturing process of both the rim and the tyre. Remember: if it's a major struggle to fit the tyre at home in a warm garage, how are you going to cope in the wind and rain of a winter's day?

Removing a tyre

1 This worn-out tyre is due for replacement. Deflate it by first removing the dust cap. On Presta tubes, unscrew the centre nut and depress the valve; on Schrader tubes, depress the valve centre with a nail or the edge of a tyre lever.

2 With the tyre deflated, push the tyre bead into the centre of the rim. Do this on both sides of the tyre. Next use a tyre lever to hook the bead over the rim. If you have a loose-fitting tyre, it may now be possible to slide the lever all the way around the rim, lifting the tyre bead over as you proceed. If not, hook the lever over a spoke and insert another tyre lever about 100mm from the first. This should be enough to get the bead over the rim, but if not insert yet another lever a little further along.

3 Once the tyre bead is over the edge of the rim, use the tyre lever or your hand to unhook the bead all the way around the rim.

4 Reach into the tyre carcass and pull down the tube all the way around.

5 When you get to the valve, push the tyre back over the rim, pull out the valve and remove the tube.

6 Now pull the tyre off the rim. You may need to use a tyre lever to help it over the rim.

7 Now is a good time to inspect the rim tape and the condition of the rim itself. On single-wall rims check that none of the spokes are standing proud of the spoke nipples. File them down if necessary.

TYRE CONSTRUCTION
This all-purpose 700c road tyre from Vittoria features several construction layers. Cross-weaving of the aramid fibres beneath the surface tread offers increased puncture protection. Suitable for use in the wet and the dry, this tyre is also available in a choice of colours and sizes.

TYRE CARCASS AND RIM TAPES

Tyres will often need changing not because they've worn out, but because the rubber has started to perish. Tyres will often perish on the sidewall first, so this should be the first point you check.

This tyre still has a few rides left in it, but the perished sidewall and escaping yarn indicate it will need replacing soon.

This mountain-bike tyre has a worn-out tread. Still fine for road use but past its best for off-road use. Compare the tread to the new one.

Plastic rim tapes are reusable, but many riders still prefer the old-style cloth tape.

Fitting a new tyre

1 Many tyres are directional, so check for an arrow mark on the sidewall. The arrow must point in the direction of travel. Lift one side of the tyre over the rim.

2 Slightly inflate the new tube – it should just about hold its shape.

3 Push over the bead at the valve hole and then push the valve through. If the tyre has a distinct logo, rotate the tyre and line it up with the valve. This makes finding the valve a little easier.

4 Tuck the tube into the tyre and then, starting at the valve, work the tyre bead over the rim with your thumbs. The bead should slip over easily until the last third.

5 Now start to stretch the tyre over the final third. Push the already fitted section down into the rim well as you progress.

6 If the tyre has stretched and dropped into the rim well, you'll be able to roll the last section of bead over the rim. Sometimes you'll have to resort to the use of a tyre lever.

7 Check that the tyre bead is seated correctly all the way around. Make sure the valve is at right angles to the rim.

8 Inflate the tyre slightly. Check that it's centralised on the rim and then inflate it some more. Roll the tyre along a hard surface to settle it completely on the rim and then fully inflate it to the correct pressure.

Tubeless tyres

Tubeless tyres are growing in popularity in mountain biking and are starting to make inroads in the road market, too. As the name implies, a tubeless system requires no inner tube. The tyre, which has an open cross-section like a clincher, and the rim are made in such a way that fitting them together provides an airtight seal. As a result, 'tubeless' is best described as a complete wheel-tyre system, rather than a wheelset or tyre individually, and is why you must buy specific tubeless tyres and wheels rather than adapt your current set-up. The wheels feature a deeper rim, while tubeless tyres come with a tougher bead and sidewalls. This combination creates an immediate sealing with the rim and a perfect fit.

Because you don't require an inner tube, tubeless can run at lower pressures than traditional tyres. This is why comfort and grip are enhanced. That lower pressure also reduces chances of blowouts,

and pinch flats are eradicated because of the lack of an inner tube. Puncture protection also comes with tubeless tyres that are filled with sealant (from all good bike shops). The sealant serves to plug cuts in the tyre of up to a pretty impressive 5mm before pressure is lost. Too great a hole and, though the sealant should get you home, you'll have to shop around for a new tubeless tyre.

Key to tubeless is the seal. This is tight fitting and requires waterproof plastic tape that's much thicker than traditional rim tape. You'll also need a track pump specific to tubeless. Instead of pumping air direct to the tyre, these store pumped air. Keep pumping to the required section on the gauge. You then connect the pump to the tyre's valve, press a button and the air gushes into your tyre at high pressure to spread the sealant and ensure a tight seal. Be warned: this job can be messy so wear appropriate clothing and perform outside…

Removing a tubeless tyre

1 Remove the valve cap. With Presta valves, unscrew and press to deflate; Schrader requires simply pressing with a thin object.

2 You might find the tyre's loose enough to begin removing from the wheel by fingers and thumbs…

3 …However, the tight fit of tyre to wheel more often than not requires use of tyre levers. These tend to be plastic or metallic. Plastic tyre levers are less likely to damage the rim or tyre

4 Once you've hooked your first tyre lever beneath the bead, hook the other end onto the nearest spoke.

5 Hook a second tyre lever near the first one – again onto the nearest spoke. This helps to ease the tyre off.

6 You can either begin removing the whole tyre with the first lever or use a third tyre lever.

7 Clean the rim strip of old sealant.

Fitting a tubeless tyre

1 Fit the wheel into the tyre and begin squeezing back into the rim.

2 Use a tyre lever to assist in easing the tyre back on. But leave a small section of tyre unattached at the bottom of the wheel.

3 Run your hands around the wheel to ensure the majority of the tyre is fitted tightly within the rim.

4 Measure out the sealant as per manufacturer's instructions and pour into the gap you left at the base of the tyre.

5 Turn the wheel upside down so that the sealant spreads to the bottom.

6 Pop the rest of the tyre on with a tyre lever.

7 Use either a tubeless track pump or canister attached to your traditional track pump to inflate the tyre to the manufacturer's recommended psi.

8 Bounce and rotate the tyre to spread the sealant equally. Once you're confident the tyre's fully seated, you can top up the pressure to suit.

TOOLS NEEDED
In addition to sealant, you'll need tyre levers. You'll also need either a dedicated tubeless track pump or a canister (Airshot, pictured) that screws onto the valve of your 'normal' track pump. Why is explained in the introduction copy.

Puncture repairs

To repair any puncture you'll need to remove the wheel and inner tube. Sometimes you may know exactly where to look for the puncture from visible damage to the tyre, but more often than not it will take some locating. Try pumping the tube up first and listen for the escaping air by holding the tube close to your ear.

The sure-fire way of locating a puncture is to place the inflated tube in a bowl of clean water and watch for the air bubbles escaping. Start at the valve and work your way slowly round the tube, wiping away any small bubbles that form on the tube as you go. If you're trying to locate a very slow puncture, be patient because these leaks may only create an air bubble very slowly. Stretching and compressing the tube under the water often helps. If you have a slow puncture, pay particular attention to previous repairs.

With the puncture located, check the tyre out. Very carefully run your hands around the inside of the tyre, feeling for any sharp objects. Examine the tread of the tyre, looking for cuts and anything embedded in it. Remove anything found. Thorns can be pulled out with pliers or pushed out from the inside of the tyre with the end of a tyre lever.

If you have a puncture away from home, the easy fix is to fit a spare tube and repair the punctured tube later. If you need to locate the hole and fix it at the roadside, you'll have to improvise a bowl of water by using a convenient puddle or by dribbling water from your drink bottle over the suspect section of the tube.

How many times can you patch a tube? Well, a puncture repair kit will always be a lot cheaper than a new tube, but a tube with six or more patches will need another puncture kit, so that may be the time to replace it. Many riders consider any repair as a temporary solution and will replace the tube as soon as they return home. However, a correctly repaired tube is as good as new, and replacing a tube after only one puncture is a waste of resources.

In recent years, self-adhesive repair patches have come on to the market. The first generation of these were poor, but the newer types provide robust and quick repairs. Various sealants are also available. These are injected into the tube and seal any punctures as they occur. They can be very effective, the only problem being when they fail and you have to resort to a traditional repair – sealant escaping from the tube makes gluing a patch in place difficult.

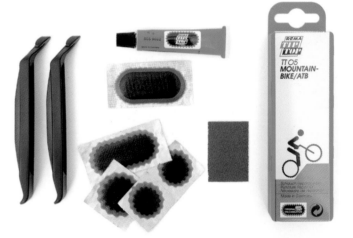

Puncture repair kits

Feather-edge patches feature in most modern puncture repair kits. Some may contain a tyre repair patch. Instant self-adhesive repair patches are an effective alternative and cut down on weight. Heavy-duty tyre repair patches are also available.

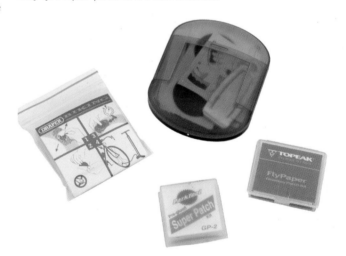

CLASSIC PUNCTURES

The classic pinhole created by a thorn or sharp object. With the tube removed, carefully check the inside of the tyre carcass. This is best done whilst wearing gloves. Remove the offending object and then check the outer surface of the tyre for any other damage.

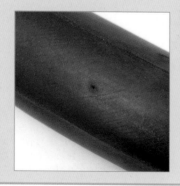

A typical 'snake bite' puncture, caused by the tyre trapping the inner tube on the rim edge after a drop, jump or striking a raised object. If this happens frequently then consider larger tyres, changing the tyre pressure or converting to a tubeless system.

Repairing punctures

1 Once you've located the puncture, align the tube with the tyre. This may give you a clue as to where to look in the tyre for a nail or thorn, for example.

2 This is a classic puncture caused by a thorn on the road from the annual autumn hedge cutting.

3 Apply a thin layer of adhesive around the hole and allow it to dry. Don't rush here because the drying of the adhesive is vital to a successful repair.

4 While the adhesive dries, check the tyre for the cause of the puncture. Here the thorn needs to be removed. Use the flat edge of a tyre lever to push it out and then pull it free from the outside.

5 When the adhesive is dry, peel off the foil backing from the patch and apply it to the tube. Press down firmly, working out from the centre.

Repairing tyres

Some puncture repair kits may be supplied with a heavy-duty tyre patch. These are applied in exactly the same manner as a tube repair patch. If you damage a tyre while out riding and don't have a suitable repair patch, it's often possible to effect a temporary repair using trail or roadside litter. Cut-up plastic drinks bottles and heavy-duty polythene bags can often be utilised as a short-term repair to get you home.

6 Stretch the patch or fold it over to release the clear covering and then peel it off, working out from the centre. After removing the clear backing, a sprinkling of chalk dust or talc will stop any excess glue sticking the inner tube to the inside of the tyre when the tube is re-fitted.

Chain and drivetrain care

Chains need proper care and attention. How often you clean and lubricate your chain will very much depend on your bike and your riding style. A classic city bike with a fully enclosed chain guard may require checking perhaps once a year. A serious off-road mountain bike will need the chain checking and lubricating after every ride, especially in the winter.

On a road bike, a chain clean and lube every 400 miles would be a rough guide, but again this will all depend on road conditions. If you only ride in dry conditions and use a dry-type oil on the chain, you may get away with less maintenance.

The best way to check chain wear is by using one of the many chain checkers on the market. These are inexpensive and give a more accurate determination of chain wear. Replace the chain as soon as the tool indicates it's worn. Leave it too long and you'll end up replacing the entire drivetrain. Chains can also fail through cracked plates/rollers or twisted links therefore a visual check is also important

The best way to clean a chain is without doubt to remove it and soak it in a suitable degreaser. You may need to repeat the process several times to thoroughly clean it. Removing the chain is simple on chains that have a removable link, but not so simple on Shimano chains as you'll require a new connector pin. (See Chapter 4 for further details.)

The most common chain problem (apart from wear) is a stiff link. This is often felt as a slight hesitation as the link moves through the jockey wheels, and may cause the chain to skip if you're in a high gear. The stiff link can be corrected with a chain tool.

Bikes fitted with indexed gears have a minor adjustment facility available at the rear derailleur (except the Shimano off-road 'Shadow' derailleurs) and many also have a barrel adjuster at the gear changer. Before making any adjustments, check the condition of the outer gear cable and the position of the rear mech. The jockey-wheel cage must be parallel to the rear sprockets or you'll never get the indexing correct.

Next, ride the bike with a mid-range gear selected. The indexing requires adjustment if you can hear the chain scrubbing against the next sprocket. Rotate the barrel adjuster anticlockwise to increase cable tension and to move the mech up the sprockets; clockwise to decrease cable tension and move the mech down the sprockets. Make minor adjustments and ride the bike between each adjustment until it's right. If your problem is the chain falling off the rear sprockets, then the 'high' and 'low' stop screws will require adjustment. These are marked 'H' and 'L'. Adjustment is fully described in Chapter 4.

Chain care

1 This style of chain cleaner is supplied with its own tin of biodegradable solvent.

2 Clamp the cleaner to the bottom of the chain and pedal backwards to clean it.

3 Use a chain checker to assess chain wear. This chain requires immediate replacement.

4 A stiff link can often be spotted as it passes the jockey wheels.

5 Use the centre guides of a chain tool to free-off a stiff link.

HOW TO USE YOUR GEARS

Low gears are for climbing hills, mid-range gears for accelerating and cruising, and high gears for flat-out speed. As a general rule, spinning along easily in a low- to mid-range gear is preferable to applying loads of power and pushing hard in a high gear.

Whilst some gear systems feature an indicator on the gear shifters to tell you what gear you're in, it's far better to get used to riding by feel rather than constantly looking at the gear selection indicator. Remember that the small sprocket at the rear is the high gear and the small chainring at the front is the low gear. Always avoid using the extremes. On a triple-chainset bike, for example, try to avoid using the large chainring at the front and the large sprocket at the rear. It places far less stress on the drivetrain if you move to the middle ring at the front and the smaller sprocket at the rear. There will be little change in the effective gear ratio if you do this.

Automatic chain cleaner

A whole host of chain cleaners are available. All rely on a set of brushes and rollers to clean the chain. Some require holding in place, others use the jockey wheel as a stop. They all require filling with a suitable solvent. Because the reservoir is small, frequent changes of fluid are required. Whilst effective they're no substitute for removing the chain and soaking it in solvent.

Rear mech

1 When the indexing requires adjustment, first locate the barrel adjusters.

2 The loop of cable where it enters the rear mech is often a cause of indexing problems. Release the inner cable and pull it free from the outer cable.

3 Wipe clean the inner, lubricate it and refit it. Select the high gear, pull the slack from the cable and tighten the cable clamp.

4 Select a mid-range gear on the rear block and check the chain position. It should lie with the teeth of the sprocket in the centre of the chain links. Rotate the barrel adjuster as needed to centralise the chain. When the indexing is correct in the middle of the block it should be correct in all gears. Some very minor adjustments may be required after a short road test.

Cleaning your bike

After a ride in the mud and rain, a bike wash and clean should be a priority. If you have the time, wash the surface mud and grime off as soon as possible. If you've had to leave it for a day then brush off the loose dirt first before damping the bike with plain clean water. Let the water soak into the grime. This is a good time to assemble all the required brushes and cleaners before washing off the muck. You'll need a bucket, sponge and brush as a minimum for cleaning. It's worthwhile investing in a couple of specialist bike brushes (or a kit) that let you get into all the nooks and crannies.

Get the worst of the grime off with plain water and then clean and degrease the chain as illustrated on the previous page. To get all the ingrained dirt off, use one of the many bike-specific cleaning products now on the market. Always follow the instructions on the bottle, as many require diluting before use.

Many cyclists don't like the idea of using a pressure washer on their bike, but if you're sensible they're useful. Just remember not to aim the hose directly at any bearings or weather seals, such as suspension fork seals.

Now is a good time to give the rims a proper clean. Use a nylon scouring pad to clean out the ingrained fragments of stone and other debris from the rims. On bikes fitted with disc brakes, carefully clean the rotors with a specialist disc brake cleaner.

A whole variety of cleaning products are available. Keep any that contain silicon away from the braking surfaces.

Specialist brushes are available, but an old toothbrush is still a useful tool.

SPECIALIST DISC BRAKE CLEANER

This specialist cleaner removes contamination from brake rotors. It can also be used to remove spilt brake fluid from the bike paintwork. This is particularly important if your hydraulic brake system uses a car-based DOT-type fluid, as this can attack the paintwork. It's also useful for deep cleaning the braking surface on rim brake wheels.

Cleaning your bike

1 If your bike is as bad as this, then remove the worst of the mud and grime with a soft brush.

2 Wash down the bike with plain water first – this will remove most of the dirt.

3 Apply a specialist bike cleaner, working it into the remaining dirt.

4 This specialist brush is used to clean dirt from the rear sprockets and chainrings.

5 A nylon scouring pad can be used to clean the rim braking surface.

6 A standard car shampoo and an old washing-up brush are suitable alternatives to specialist cleaners and brushes.

7 Wash off the bike cleaner with fresh water. On a really dirty bike you may have to go over it again with a brush and more cleaner.

8 Use a water-dispersing product to drive the water from the drivetrain, and then dry the bike with a clean cloth.

Quick lube routine

The drivetrain is the most important part of the bike that needs to be constantly checked and lubricated. The front wheel constantly throws up muck and water from the road, which tends to stick to a well-oiled chain and then starts to work its way into the chain links and sprocket teeth. So always focus on the drivechain first, cleaning it if necessary before lubricating it.

How often you lube the drivetrain (and other components) will depend on how often you use your bike and the conditions you ride in. Winter rides will always demand more lubrication than the occasional summer ride. Bikes kept outside may well require lubrication before every ride if they're only used occasionally, while the keen mountain-biker will clean and lube their bike after every ride.

A bewildering array of bicycle lubricants are now on the market. Chain lubes are often described as 'wet' or 'dry'. Most will claim to have a high-tech formula with the addition of various exotic compounds and waxes. Some boast the use of 'nano-ceramic chemistry', others claim to have 'Teflon surface protection'. No doubt all these claims are true, but for the average rider the difference between one lube and another may not be apparent in the real world. A dry type of lube may be the best choice for many. These use a solvent that evaporates after penetrating the chain links, leaving behind a slippery dry surface. This has the advantage of preventing dirt from sticking to the chain.

A lubricant with a wax base should be used on cables as aerosol lubricants or lubricants with a standard petrochemical or Teflon/PTFE base can break down the liner in outer cables.

The rest of the lubrication points on the bike don't require such a high-tech approach. A general purpose oil will suffice here.

Lubrication

1 The chain and sprockets are a priority, but don't lubricate a dirty drivetrain.

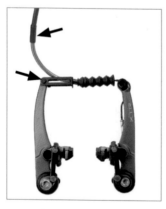

2 Oil the pivot points. Unhook the 'noodle' and thoroughly lubricate with a wax-based lubricant.

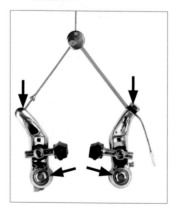

3 Cantilever brakes require lubrication on the pivots and at the straddle wire.

4 Rear derailleurs require a light lubrication at the pivots. A small drop on the barrel adjuster is also a good idea.

SLOTS AND STOPS
Most modern bikes have slotted cable guides. Where possible remove the cable from the guide to lubricate the inner.

5 Jockey wheels require lubrication with a chain oil.

6 Front derailleurs require lubrication of the pivots.

7 Brake lever pivots should be lubricated with a wax-based lubricant. Where possible remove the cable, hold it up and dribble oil down the inner.

8 All exposed inner cables should be lubricated with a wax-based lubricant. Where possible remove the cables from the stops to lube the inner cable.

CHAPTER

BRAKING SYSTEMS

Types of brake

Although very different in design, all the brakes shown on this page work by pressing a brake pad against a braking surface. Their effectiveness depends on how hard the pad is forced against the rim or disc, and how well the pad material bites. This varies with different combinations of materials, as does the rate at which the pad wears. For the best braking performance with rim brakes, always specify the material that the rim is made of when buying new pads. Most replacement rim brake pads are manufactured from various polyurethane compounds. These pads combine good braking with a low rate of wear.

Disc brake pads are available in a variety of compounds, usually described as 'sintered' or 'organic'. Within these two broad categories are a host of variants, each with specific properties dependent on their intended use. As a general guide, organic brake pads are for general use in most conditions while sintered pads are a harder type for longer life in abrasive conditions.

Don't forget that the braking surface of the rim or disc also wears; not as fast as the brake pads, but it can eventually get so bad that the wheel or disc collapses without warning. As a precaution, always check the rim when you fit new rim brake pads. If the rim is worn, replace the wheel; if it's a quality wheel, consider replacing the rim. On disc brakes check the thickness of the disc. The minimum thickness may be marked on it but, if not, you'll have to consult the manufacturer.

Cantilever brakes

Once popular, these have now been superseded by the V brake and dual-pivot brake. Lightweight and powerful, they're still to be found on cyclo cross, old touring and mountain bikes.

Dual-pivot brakes

These are now common on road bikes and light touring bikes. Each arm moves independently and, when set up correctly, they require little maintenance. Most incorporate some type of release mechanism to allow easy wheel removal. All feature a form of brake-pad height adjustment to accommodate different rims.

V brakes

Now standard on lower-priced mountain bikes and many commuter bikes. They allow the use of large-volume tyres and, when set up correctly, are very powerful. The top-of-the-range models feature a parallel pad operating system that keeps the pad-to-rim angle constant.

Hub brakes

Popular on the Continent, where they're used on city or commuter bikes. Many incorporate hub gears and dynamos. They're often fitted with a 'coaster' brake system, which is operated by pedalling backwards. A very low-maintenance brake.

Disc brakes

Originally only for mountain bikes, they're now also popular on cyclocross, commuter and touring bikes, and they're beginning to permeate the world of road bikes, too. They're low-maintenance and very powerful. Available with either hydraulic or cable operation, they're not affected by a buckled or distorted rim and are also less affected by weather and wet/muddy conditions.

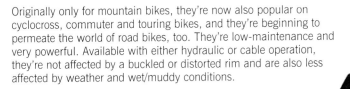

Inspection and lubrication

For cable-operated rim brakes there will always be a certain amount of slack in the cables before the brake blocks start to touch the rim. This is because there must be clearance between the rim and the blocks. The cable outers will also compress as the brake pads start to bite on the rim. When correctly adjusted, the brakes should be fully on well before the brake lever contacts the handlebars.

As the brake pads wear down, the travel at the lever will increase. Once the brake lever starts to get too close to the handlebars, adjustment will be required and possibly cable replacement. Because all rim brakes (apart from parallel-push V brakes and hydraulically operated rim brakes) travel through an arc as they operate, close attention should be paid to the position of the pads on the rim as they wear. Worn and poorly adjusted rim brakes can drop below the rim and into the spokes, with disastrous consequences.

Hydraulic disc brakes suffer from none of these problems. Depending on the make and design, some increase in lever travel may be noticeable. Many now feature the ability to adjust the initial starting position (or reach) of the lever and the 'bite point' – the amount of travel before the pads start to contact the brake disc.

Test, inspect and adjust

1 Pull on the lever and check for excessive play. If it touches the handlebars, attention is required. On cheaper brakes the lever may never feel rock solid – there will always be a slightly 'soft' feel to them. Inspect the lever pivot bolt and the security of the brake clamp fixing. Also check cables and casings for damage and wear.

2 Check the pads for wear and contamination. Most pads will have a minimum thickness mark on them. If the pad has been missing the rim slightly and a ridge line has formed, this can always be trimmed off with a sharp knife and the pad repositioned, providing there's plenty of friction material left on the pad.

3 On bikes with flat or riser handlebars, adjustment is made at the brake lever. Undo the locking ring and screw the barrel adjuster out (anticlockwise) to take up the slack in the cable. Never unscrew the adjuster all the way – at least four threads should be left in the lever body. Tighten up the locking ring, making sure that the slots in the ring, adjuster and brake *do not* line up.

4 On road bikes and some other bikes, adjustment is carried out at the brake. Release the lock nut and unscrew the barrel adjuster to bring the brake pads closer to the rim. Cantilever brakes will require adjustment by altering of the pad position or via the cable locking nut.

5 Hydraulic disc brakes can often be adjusted for reach and bite point. Check the security of the brake and caliper mounting points. The heat generated by disc brakes seems to make them more vulnerable to bolts coming loose. They may have locking wire and locking washers fitted to prevent this.

6 On hydraulic brakes, pull the lever hard and check for fluid leaks. Pay particular attention to the hose fittings. Check the hoses for damage and wear.

Brake lubrication

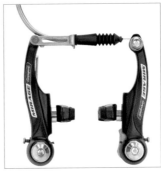

1 If the frame has slotted cable guides, pull the cables free and slide the outers down. You may need to open the quick release to free the cable. Oil the inner cable and slide the outer up and down to drag oil into the outer cable. On cantilever and V brakes, lubricate the return spring and pivot mounts.

2 On V brakes, lubricate the front and rear of the pivots. Because of the bend in the 'noodle' (see right) it's a favourite place for the cable to stiffen up, so pull the noodle free and slide it down to the clamp nut to expose the inner cable. Clean and lubricate the inner cable.

THE BRAKING SURFACE

Wheel rims do wear out, so they should be part of any braking-system inspection. All rims start life with a flat surface but, as they wear, they tend to develop a concave profile. Some may have a wear-line marked – as soon as this limit is reached the line fades and the rim should be replaced. A quick check is to hold a straight edge against the rim and try to assess the remaining thickness. If you can flex the brake surface with strong thumb pressure, it's almost certainly due for replacement.

When fitting new brake pads, make sure you know the rim material. Most rims are an aluminium alloy, but plated steel rims may appear on cheaper bikes and are still popular on BMX models. The increasingly popular carbon rims work better with carbon brake pads to reduce heat on the rim. Some rims may have a ceramic coating applied to the braking surface to improve braking in the wet. Each type of rim needs a specific brake pad to match, so be sure to fit compatible pads.

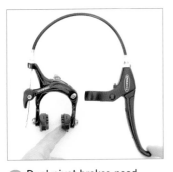

3 Dual-pivot brakes need lubrication at the pivots, the centre mounting and the cable clamp bolt. Lubricate the pivot at the brake lever. If you're working on a bike with drop handlebars, peel back the lever hoods to access the pivot.

4 On disc brakes, lubricate the lever pivot. If you think the pistons are sticking then remove the wheel and brake pads. With care, apply a little lubricant to the exposed pistons. Push the pistons back into the caliper and refit the pads and wheel.

Quick releases

V brakes should be set up so that it's a bit of a struggle to release the metal pipe (or 'noodle' as it's often called) from the arm. It's often easier to just pull the noodle free from the cable holder whilst pushing in the arm of the brake.

On cantilever brakes, compress both arms and unhook the straddle wire. If you encounter difficulty you may have to release the tension first by screwing in the barrel adjuster at the brake lever. Some bikes may also have an adjuster below the handlebars or behind the seat pinch bolt.

OIL

Oil and braking surfaces do not mix, so take care when lubricating the brakes. Take care using aerosol lubricants or stick to the good old-fashioned oil can or bottle. Always hold a clean rag under the brake if you think there might be any chance of oil dripping on to the rim or brake block. Wipe down the brake with a clean cloth when you're finished.

5 On cantilever brakes, lubricate the pivots at the front and rear. A dab of grease on the straddle-wire quick release stops it seizing and helps prevent any annoying squeaks from developing.

Most single- and dual-pivot brakes have a cam system fitted close to the cable lock nut. Rotate the cam and the brakes move away from the rim.

Some road-bike brakes have the release built into the brake lever. These Campagnolo levers have a push-button system that resets itself the first time you pull on the brakes.

V brakes

Originally developed by Shimano to replace cantilever and U brakes on mountain bikes, V brakes are common on lower-end mountain bikes and some commuter bikes. The 'V' name is believed to derive from the fact Shimano developed it after the U brake, which was a type of cantilever brake fitted to the chain stays on early mountain bikes and BMXs.

V brakes are direct-acting or linear brakes – the amount of movement on the lever is exactly the same at the brake. They're powerful, low-maintenance brakes that can accommodate a variety of tyre sizes. They're a simple upgrade for any bike with cantilever brakes, as long as a few things are considered: the mounting bosses must be 80mm from centre to centre, they must be fitted with compatible brake levers and they must clear any bike rack or mudguards fitted.

The fitting of new cables and brake pads is covered on pages 55–59 of this manual.

V brakes: strip and adjustment

1 Release the locking bolt and pull off the rubber boot. Unhook the noodle pipe and pull it off the brake cable. Remove the wheel if you've not already done so.

2 Unbolt and remove the mounting bolts. Clean the brake boss on the bike frame. Most bosses are screwed into the frame mountings, so check the security of these. Tighten the bosses if necessary.

3 Clean the V brake and check the condition of the return spring. Use a small amount of grease to lubricate the brake boss.

4 Refit the brake arm. Position of spring into the holes on the brake boss depends on the strength of the spring in the brake.

5 Refit the bolt and tighten to the correct torque if available. Hook the long arm of the spring over the brake arm and check that it springs back when pushed in.

7 Release the noodle pipe and refit the wheel. Hook the brake cable noodle back in. If this isn't possible it may be necessary to release the locking bolt and slacken the cable slightly. Adjust the cable so that it's just possible to hook and unhook it.

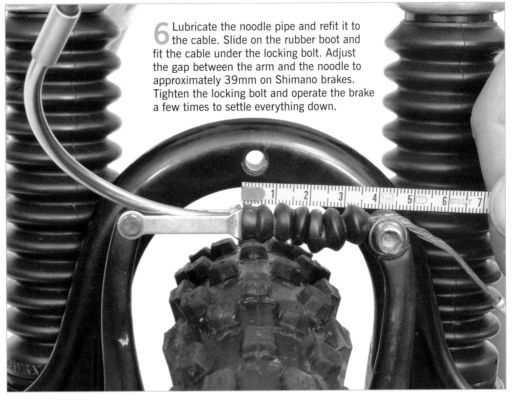

6 Lubricate the noodle pipe and refit it to the cable. Slide on the rubber boot and fit the cable under the locking bolt. Adjust the gap between the arm and the noodle to approximately 39mm on Shimano brakes. Tighten the locking bolt and operate the brake a few times to settle everything down.

8 With the wheel in the frame the brakes should now be balanced. Use the tension adjusting screw to equalise the gap between the pad and the rim. Operate the brake between each adjustment. If the brakes can't be balanced with the tension screw, try moving the position of the spring mounting in the frame to the upper or lower hole as required.

TIP:
Sometimes the cable boot on a V brake can crumple making the brake feel spongy when the brake is applied. Some mechanics will shorten or even remove this boot in order to make the brake feel positive again.

BRAKE LEVERS

The angle of the lever can be adjusted. The exact angle is very much a personal choice, but avoid having your wrist bent up or down excessively. A good starting point is to sit on the bike and put your arm out straight, in the normal riding position, and adjust the brake lever so that your wrist drops ever so slightly.

Most levers have the facility to adjust the reach. This is often a small grub screw. Move it in or out to alter the reach. Aim to set the lever up so that it falls naturally to hand.

WHEN YOU NEED TO DO THIS:
- When upgrading from standard cantilevers.
- When the arms fail to spring back from the rim of the brake as they're released. Don't confuse this with a seized or worn brake cable.

TIME:
- Allow two hours for a full brake clean, strip and upgrade if necessary.

DIFFICULTY:
- It can take a while to set the arms up correctly, especially if you're trying to keep to the 39mm gap recommended by Shimano for their V brakes.

Dual-pivot brakes

Dual-pivot brakes are now common on the majority of road bikes and, as such, it's important to know how to replace them. When removing this type of brake, carefully note the position of the various washers and spacers. They are important. If any parts are missing or damaged on cheaper brakes, it's often less expensive to replace the complete caliper, as spare parts may well be hard to find.

The biggest issue you may face is centring them in relation to the rim. Trial and error fitting may be required to find the sweet spot where the caliper remains clear of the rim and more or less centred in the frame or fork.

WHEN YOU NEED TO DO THIS:
- When the brake action becomes stiff, even after fitting new cables.
- When the arms fail to spring back from the rim as the brake is released. Don't confuse this with a seized or worn brake cable.

TIME:
- Allow two hours for a full brake clean, strip and upgrade if necessary.

DIFFICULTY: 🔧🔧🔧
- It can take a while to centralise the calipers correctly. As a general rule, cheap side-pull brakes will take longer to set up than a quality set of dual-pivot brakes.

Dual-pivot brakes: strip and adjustment

1 Most dual-pivot brakes are held in place with a recessed hex-headed bolt. A long hex key may be required to reach the mounting bolt.

2 Fit the wheel and then align the brake pads. This is best achieved by using your hand to compress the caliper arms against the wheel rim.

3 Next centralise the caliper arms and pads over the wheel. Aim to get the gap between the pad and the rim equal on both sides.

4 Fit the brake cable. Pull it tight whilst compressing the brake with one hand if necessary and then tighten the cable fixing bolt.

5 Operate the brake a few times and adjust the cable tension as necessary. Fine-tune the position of the brake arms with the small grub screw so that the pads are exactly the same distance from the braking surface on both sides of the wheel.

6 Finally, finish the job by fitting a new cable end fitting, crimping it firmly into place with a pair of pliers.

Fitting new brake cables

Replacing the cables is a very similar task on all cable-operated brakes, regardless of type. Brake cable inners are usually 1.5 or 1.6mm in diameter. They may be galvanised steel, plain steel or stainless steel, and may have a special coating applied to reduce friction. Two types of (lever) end fitting are commonly used: the pear shape and the flat disc. Flat-bar bikes tend to use the disc fitting and drop-bar bikes the pear-shaped fitting.

Brake cable outers are normally spiral-wound steel or stainless steel cables with a plastic coating. They're available in a range of colours and are often sold by the metre. Some have an inner liner or are coated with a friction-reducing material – often polytetrafluoroethylene, better know as PTFE or by the trade name 'Teflon'. If you're fitting PTFE-coated cables *do not* apply any additional lubricant – PTFE is a very low-friction material and requires no further lubrication.

If you're only replacing the inner cable, use a quality stainless steel type. Lubricate the inner cable with a wax-based lubricant as you feed it through the outer cable.

If you're replacing both the inner and outer cables, there are several makes of complete cable kits on the market. These often use Teflon-lined cables and come complete with the required ferrules and end fittings. Possibly not worth the expense on a bike that sees only occasional use, but well worth it on a bike that's used regularly.

Adjusting the cables when they've been replaced may require a little trial and error. One tip is to tie the brake lever up with a tie wrap or similar and leave it under tension for an hour or so. This fully compresses the fittings and stretches the cable. You should then only need to adjust the cables once.

CABLE PULLER
Not essential, but very useful when dealing with side-pull and dual-pull brakes.

Fitting new V brake cables

1 Release the cable clamp nut and pull the inner cable free. Pull off the rubber boot and cable guide pipe (or 'noodle' pipe).

3 If you're replacing the outer cables, remove them one at a time. Use each one as a template to cut new outers to the correct length, using an engineer's file if necessary to square the end of the new outer cable. Always replace the end fittings.

5 Always fit a new brake noodle and feed the new inner through it. Slide on the rubber boot and slip the cable under the clamp bolt. Note that noodles have different bends, normally 90° for the rear and around 135° for the front.

2 Line up the slots on the barrel adjuster and free the cable. Unhook it from the lever. On some models the cable end fitting is hidden behind a cover.

4 Fit the new inner cable to the brake lever and feed it through the outer cable. Wind out the barrel adjuster a few turns, making sure the cable slot is not in line with the lever slot.

6 Press the brake pads against the rim, pull the cable tight and tighten the clamp bolt. Screw in the barrel adjuster and pull the brakes on a few times to settle the cables. Check that the noodle can be released from the brake. Further minor adjustment may be needed.

Fitting new dual-pivot cables

1 A frayed cable will require replacement. Broken strands can unravel and soon work their way into the outer cable.

2 Cut the cable above the frayed section. Undo the locking nut and pull the frayed cable out.

3 Release the inner cable at the lever and pull it free from the outer. Fit the new cable, pull it tight and tighten the clamp bolt.

4 Return the quick release to its normal position and unscrew the adjuster a few turns. Press the brake pads against the rim, loosen the cable and pull through any slack. Tighten the cable clamp locking bolt and screw in the adjuster.

5 Some minor adjustment of the cable may be necessary. When complete cut the cable to length and fit a crimp.

Internal brake cables

Internal brake cables – in other words, where the brake cable's routed within the frame rather than externally – are increasingly seen on all genres of bikes, be it road, mountain bike or commuting. The primary reason for this is aesthetic. Concealing the jumble of cables tidies things up nicely, leaving your curved frame to take centre stage.

But there are also practical reasons, the main one being that by hiding away your cables, you're actually protecting them. This means they should not only work more proficiently, but last longer, too.

The problem is, they're trickier to maintain. But, as you'll see, key is a thin stretch of plastic tubing. Fail to use this and you'll be playing around with magnets to try and locate your new brake cable!

1 The first step to removing the old brake cable is by unscrewing the bolt on the cable clamp. This commonly requires a 4mm or 5mm Allen key.

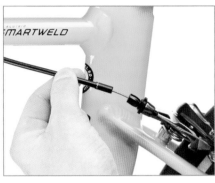

2 Once the brake cable is released from the clamp, simply ease it out.

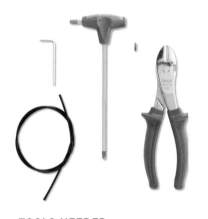

TOOLS NEEDED
For this job you'll need cable cutters, a length of plastic tubing (cable guide), and 2mm and 4mm or 5mm Allen keys.

3 You then need to unscrew the grub screw where the cable exits the top tube.

4 You can now undo the outer cable that keeps the inner cable neatly tucked away in the top tube. You might have to do this at the saddle end, too.

5 Remove the ferrule off the end of the outer cable because that won't fit through the frame hole. Put it somewhere safe as you'll need it again later.

6 Slide on a stretch of thin plastic tubing, which you can purchase from most bike shops.

7 This plastic tubing goes over the inner cable and pushes the current outer cable out of the frame.

8 Pull new plastic tubing out of the top tube. You can then slide the new brake cable through the plastic tubing. Remove plastic tubing, add outer and connect brakes.

Fitting and adjusting new brake pads

Always check the condition of the wheel rim before fitting new brake pads. Grooves and a slightly concave profile are normal. Buckles and dents in the braking surface will cause problems. If you have any doubts about the condition of the rim, get a second opinion from a qualified mechanic at the local bike shop.

If the rim is so worn that it needs replacing, first consider the quality and condition of the spoke and hubs. If you have cheap wheels it will never be worth replacing the rim, and a new wheel will always be the best option. If you're riding a commuter bike or mountain bike and a new wheel is needed, consider buying one with a hub suitable for disc brakes. Wheels with IS (International Standard) disc-brake mountings and a rim with a braking surface are available, so you don't need to upgrade the brakes straight away.

Before fitting new brake pads it's always worth cleaning the rim. Use bike cleaner and a nylon scouring pad to lightly abrade the surface. Finish the job by degreasing the surface with a little brake cleaner absorbed into a clean cloth.

A bewildering range of brake pads are available. Most claim to offer improved braking power and reduced wear. Some offer wet-weather compounds or water-dispersant grooves, or both. However, if you're happy with your current brakes' performance, replacing like with like is the best place to start. If you change to another brand to improve performance, you may notice a different feel to the brakes, but hopefully there will also be an increase in stopping power. Sometimes, however, changing brake pads can lead to poor and often noisy brakes, generally resulting from a poor combination of brake pad compound and rim wear or construction. Often the only solution is an alternative set of pads.

Normally all brake pads are replaced with a small amount of 'toe-in'. This is where the front of the pad – the leading edge – meets the rim first as the brakes are applied. This minimises brake judder and squeal. Some pads are supplied with a small lip that sets the toe-in automatically. Most pads will also have a wear indicator line marked on them, as well as a direction arrow. Cartridge pads are the easiest to change, as in theory the toe-in doesn't require adjustment. These are a cost-effective upgrade for most brakes.

BEDDING IN NEW BRAKE PADS

After fitting new brake pads it will take a while for full braking efficiency to be restored. This is especially true of disc brake pads. Operating the brakes several times whilst gently freewheeling downhill will help the new pads to bed in. Some manufacturers supply brake pads with a slightly abrasive coating to assist with this process. The coating cleans the rim braking surface and quickly wears off the brake block itself.

WHEN YOU NEED TO DO THIS:
■ When the brake pads are worn.
■ If the brake friction surface becomes glazed, or if you're replacing the wheels. Never fit old brake pads to new wheels.

TIME:
■ Allow two hours for a full brake pad replacement.

DIFFICULTY: ⚲⚲
■ Straightforward on quality dual-pivot brakes, but it can be difficult to get cantilever and V brakes 'just so'.

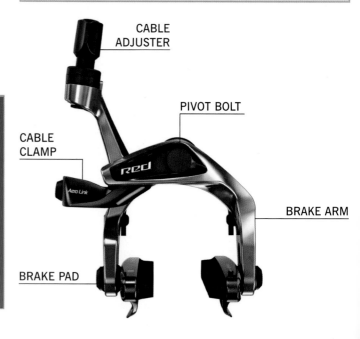

CABLE ADJUSTER

PIVOT BOLT

CABLE CLAMP

BRAKE ARM

BRAKE PAD

Fitting new pads

DUAL-PIVOT BRAKES

1 Screw in the cable adjuster and operate the quick-release mechanism. Hold the brake pad and unscrew it. Some will use a hex-headed nut whilst others will have a standard nut. On some models it's easier if the wheel is removed first.

2 Fit the new pad and hold it in place against the rim as the retaining nut is tightened. Check that the pad meets the rim squarely. On cheaper side-pull brakes it's possible to adjust the toe-in by twisting the brake arm with an adjustable spanner.

V BRAKES

V brakes have a series of adjustable washers to aid alignment and throw. These are of a different thickness and can be swapped over from each side of the brake arm to move the brake pad in or out from the rim.

HYDRAULIC DISC BRAKES

The procedure for replacing hydraulic disc brake pads is covered on page 64.

ALTERNATIVE PAD ADJUSTMENT METHOD

Clean the rim and either tape a small piece of card to it or wrap several layers of insulating tape round it. The card or tape should be no thicker than 1mm. Fit the new brake pad and tighten the retaining nut so that the pad can still be moved.

Use a tie wrap and pull the brake on so that the brake pads just contact the wheel rim. Adjust the pad by pushing it against the rim. Tighten the adjusting nut and then turn the wheel. Check that the pad meets the rim correctly. Release the brake and use the barrel adjuster to fine-tune the bite point.

Brake pad adjustment

After fitting new brake pads, they'll need fine adjustment to set their position and toe-in. The brake pad must hit the rim squarely, with the leading edge touching it slightly before the full length of the pad meets the rim. This is called 'toe-in'. Setting the toe-in correctly helps to eliminate brake squeal and judder.

Never the easiest of jobs, the task of fitting and adjusting new brake pads is more of a fiddle than a complex procedure. You may well end up having to adjust the pad position, the cable tension and the caliper position to set up the new pads perfectly.

1 Check that the new pads are correctly fitted and just nip up the securing bolt (or nut). Now adjust the pad so that the front is clear of the rim by 1mm and the rear by 2mm.

2 Pull the brake on gently and check that the pad hits the rim squarely. It should meet the rim about 1 to 2mm below the top.

3 Release the brake and pull it on again. Now check that the whole face of the pad hits the rim cleanly. Adjust it if necessary.

Brake levers

Flat-bar bikes all tend to have similar levers, held in place by a single clamp bolt or, on some models, a pair of bolts and a removable plate. Unless they're part of a combined brake and gear shifter system, they're easy to move to your preferred position. Cheaper brake levers are often thermoplastic and may have little or no adjustment possibilities. More expensive levers will be made from aluminium alloy and have a reach adjustment fitted.

Drop-handlebar levers are made from pressed aluminium alloy on the very cheap models, through cast and machined aluminium right up to carbon fibre on top-of-the-range models. Traditional levers have the cable exiting from the top, but on newer levers the cable exits from the side and is then tucked away beneath the bar tape. On all drop-handlebar levers the position must be adjusted before fitting the bar tape. Again, the positioning of the lever is very much a matter of personal preference, but is usually based on the most comfortable position for your hands on the hoods, not on the ease of using the lever.

Road-bike levers

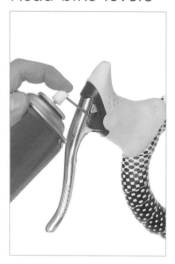

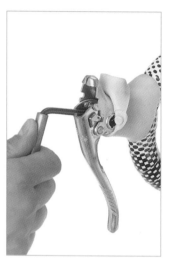

1 Lubricate the pivot point and the cable end fitting. Pull the brake on to access the cable end.

2 Release the cable at the caliper to access the lever mounting screw. Some use a screw fitting, others have a hex-headed bolt. Do not over-tighten the fixing bolt.

3 It's possible to remove a traditional lever to replace the hood by removing the fixing completely. Remove the cable clamp bolt at the caliper and then take off the lever complete with the inner cable. A new inner cable may be required.

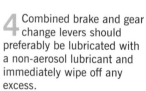

4 Combined brake and gear change levers should preferably be lubricated with a non-aerosol lubricant and immediately wipe off any excess.

Flat-bar levers

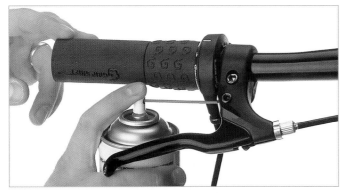

1 Lubricate the pivot point and the cable end fitting. If possible try and get some wax-based lubricant down the inner cable. A drop of oil on the threads of the barrel adjuster is also a good idea.

2 Loosen the clamp bolt to rotate the lever. If you wish to access the gear shifter, on some systems you'll need to move the brake lever. Do not over-tighten the fixing bolt.

3 Quality levers will always have some method of adjusting the distance between lever and handlebar to reduce the lever reach and accommodate smaller hands.

4 Reach, angle and the distance from the end of the handlebars are all personal choices. A starting point is to have the lever so that the first joint of your fingers lays over it with your hands on the ends of the handlebars. Adjust the angle so that the wrists are straight or slightly lowered when riding.

WHEN YOU NEED TO DO THIS:
- Lubricate the levers on mountain bikes after every ride.
- On drop-handlebar bikes the best time to alter and adjust the brake levers is when the cables are having a full overhaul.

TIME:
- Allow ten minutes or so to lubricate the levers.

DIFFICULTY:
- The fixings on drop-handlebar brakes can be more awkward to access.

Disc brakes

Disc brakes dominate the worlds of mountain bike and cyclocross, and are becoming more popular on commuting bikes and folding bikes because of their impressive stopping power, especially in the wet. The majority of major bike manufacturers have even rolled out road ranges that replace typical dual-pivot calipers with disc brakes, albeit the UCI (cycling's international governing body) are currently trialling them due to concerns about rotor discs scything professionals in high-speed mass crashes. That said, it seems only a matter of time before Froome, Nibali and co are riding bikes equipped with discs. And when they do, they'll have two models to choose from: simple cable-operated models and hydraulically operated brakes, adorned with simple solid rotors, floating rotors and even vented rotors.

So what's the difference? Firstly, fundamentally they operate the same way. Pressure is applied on the brake lever that activates pistons to push brake pads against the rotor. The difference derives from how that lever force is transferred to the caliper and brake rotor. Cable-actuated brakes operate in a similar way to rim brakes, relying on a steel cable to move the piston.

Hydraulic disc brakes, on the other hand, employ a sealed fluid-filled system as the means of actuation. This has several advantages over the cable system: greater consistency of braking due to less friction; the fluid hose can be routed around complex suspension frames with no loss of braking power; and there's no cable to seize up and create extra drag. Most modern designs are also self-adjusting. The installation, checking, bleeding and replacement of hydraulic brakes is covered on pages 64–65.

For both cable and hydraulic brakes it's important that the spokes, hub and rim are all in good condition. A wheel that's out of true or has some minor rim damage will not be an issue. However, the braking force generated at the rotor has to be transmitted to the tyre via the hub, spokes, rim and tyre, and this force is considerable, so missing or damaged spokes could lead to failure of the wheel.

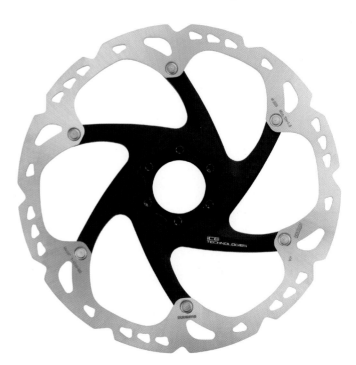

IS standard discs (or rotors) are held in place with six bolts.

Shimano's centre-lock system uses a single fixing that requires a special tool to install the disc. This is the same tool used for rear freehub cassettes.

Disc brake mounts

When you find the disc brake of your choice and wish to make a purchase it's essential that you ensure the brake has the correct mounting system for your frame and fork. The measurement of disc brake mounts is based on the distance in millimetres between the centre of the two-bolt mounting holes. If your bike has a specific mount and you wish to install disc brakes with a different mounting system you can purchase a disc brake mount adaptor. There are three main types of disc brake mounts: IS mounts, post mounts and flat mounts. The latter are becoming more popular because they allow for a neater 'footprint'.

A typical post-mount adaptor and hydraulic brake.

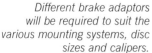

Different brake adaptors will be required to suit the various mounting systems, disc sizes and calipers.

ADJUSTING CABLE DISC BRAKE PADS

The exact method of adjustment will depend on the model of brake fitted. The brake shown in the sequence opposite requires an 8mm spanner to undo the lock nut. With the lock nut freed off, use a 2.5mm hex key to adjust the brake-pad clearance on the rotor. Operate the brake a few times and readjust the clearance if necessary. Counter-hold the 2.5mm hex key and tighten the 8mm lock nut when you're happy with the operation of the brake. Note that it's perfectly normal to feel a slight drag from the pads as the wheel is rotated.

Cable disc brakes: checking and adjustment

1 Open the quick release or remove the thru-axle and gently pull the wheel free, taking care not to damage the brake rotor. It may be necessary to back off the brake pads to allow the wheel to be removed cleanly.

2 On this style of cable-operated disc brake you'll need to use a spanner to counter-hold the cable locking bolt in order to remove the cable. This needs to be done whenever the brake pads are removed and replaced.

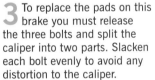

3 To replace the pads on this brake you must release the three bolts and split the caliper into two parts. Slacken each bolt evenly to avoid any distortion to the caliper.

4 With the caliper split into two, lever free the brake pad spring, taking care not to lose or distort it.

5 Tap or pick out the old pad. Inspect it for wear and clean the pad housing with a specialist brake cleaner.

6 Apply a tiny amount of copper-based anti-seize compound to the rear of the new pads and fit them into the caliper, taking care to align them properly.

7 Refit the caliper complete with the new brake pads, and then refit the three mounting bolts, tightening them evenly and in diagonal sequence.

8 Before refitting the wheel check that the caliper moves freely on the sprung mountings. If necessary, carefully lubricate the sliding pivots. Refit the front wheel and adjust the brake-pad clearance.

WHEN YOU NEED TO DO THIS:
■ It's worth stripping out the pads every six months or so to check that they're not excessively worn.
■ When the pads are worn and brake lever travel is excessive.

TIME:
■ This will depend on how the pads are retained in the caliper. Some pads are easy to change in a matter of minutes, others that require the caliper to be stripped apart can take an hour or so.

DIFFICULTY: 🔧
■ A straightforward job. The only problem you're likely to encounter is adjusting the position of the pads in the caliper.

Hydraulic disc brakes

Hydraulic disc brakes are the ultimate braking system for bikes. They offer powerful braking with very little effort required by the rider. The brake hose can be routed around the most complex frame with no frictional losses. Even a slightly buckled wheel isn't a problem. Perhaps their biggest disadvantage is their weight, though that's improved greatly over the past couple of years.

Most use standard glycol-based car brake fluid for their hydraulics, the notable exception being Shimano, who use a mineral-type fluid in their disc brakes. Never mix the two and always use the correct one for your specific system. When working with the automotive fluids (DOT 4 or DOT 5.1 are those commonly used) take precautions against spillages, as these fluids are mild paint strippers. Clean up any spills immediately with a specialist brake cleaner. We recommend that you wear gloves and eye protection at all times.

Once set up, the most common jobs on disc brakes are changing the pads and bleeding the system. Unlike rim brakes, where there's a limited number of pad types, you'll find a vast array of disc-brake pad styles and fitting methods. Most are retained by a pin system but some use a clip-on system. Add to this the specific pad shape and the three most common pad materials (sintered, organic and Kevlar) and replacing the pads can become complicated. The best advice is always to take the old pad with you to your local bike shop to obtain the correct replacement.

Bleeding the brakes can also be a complicated affair. On systems with a traditional bleed nipple, all that's required for most is a supply of fluid, a length of clear plastic hose and a small container. On systems with no bleed nipple, a special bleeding kit will be required, generally consisting of a pair of syringes, a clear plastic hose, hose clamps and adaptors to fit the brake caliper.

Glycol brake fluid tends to absorb moisture over time. Deciding when to bleed the brakes and change the fluid will depend on how long has elapsed since they were last bled and how much use they've had. Two to three years is possibly the maximum time that should pass between fluid changes. If in doubt, or if the brakes develop a spongy feeling or the lever travel is excessive, then a brake bleed and fluid change is the first thing to consider.

Bleeding hydraulic brakes

1 Loosen the brake master cylinder clamp, rotate it to the horizontal position and remove the reservoir cover.

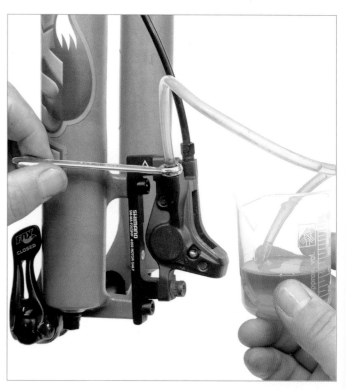

2 Remove the brake pads and push the pistons fully home. Remove the bleed nipple cover and attach a length of clear plastic hose to the nipple. Slacken off the nipple. Squeeze the brake lever fully, close the bleed nipple, release the lever and repeat.

BLEEDING TIPS

Bleeding hydraulic brakes can be very problematic, depending on the make of brake fitted. If you experience difficulty removing all the air from the system, try the following:

- While bleeding the brake, gently tap the brake hose and caliper to dislodge any trapped air bubbles.
- Consider reverse-bleeding using a syringe to push fluid up to the master cylinder.
- Remove the caliper while bleeding and rotate it to try to release any trapped air pockets in the caliper body.

- Remove the caliper and bleed the brake with the caliper higher than the master cylinder.
- Fabricate a small block of wood of the correct dimensions to keep the pistons fully retracted and try bleeding again.
- Use a tie wrap to secure the brake lever to the handlebars, remove the reservoir cap and leave the bike to stand overnight. This can often allow small bubbles to migrate up the hose to the reservoir.
- Some brake systems require particular procedures. In these cases always refer to the manufacturer's instructions specific to that product.

3 Keeping the reservoir topped up at all times, pump the brake lever until clear fluid free of bubbles emerges from the bleed hose.

4 Do not allow the level in the reservoir to drop at any time – continue to top it up as the brakes are bled. The aid of an assistant is helpful here.

5 When bleeding is complete, tighten the bleed nipple. Top up the reservoir fully and roll the seal into position. Refit the reservoir cover.

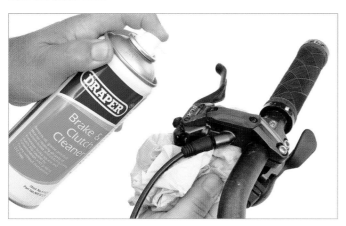

6 Use a suitable brake cleaner to wipe off any spilt brake fluid. This is especially important on braking systems that use car-type DOT fluid.

7 These Avid brakes do not have a conventional bleed nipple. You must remove the small torx-headed grub screw and fit the specialist bleed hose.

8 On this type of brake a syringe is fitted and the new fluid is pushed up the caliper to the master cylinder to bleed the system and expel any air.

Fitting new discs

1 Thoroughly clean the disc mounting surface. Check the threaded holes are clean and not damaged.

2 Use brake cleaner to wipe any anti-rust coating from the new disc. The disc must be fitted the correct way round – the arrow shows the direction of rotation.

3 The bolts (often torx-headed) are usually supplied with thread locking compound already on them; if not apply some. Note that Shimano discs are also supplied with locking washers. Line the disc up and fit all the bolts finger-tight.

4 Tighten the bolts evenly and progressively, working on each opposite pair as you go. Tighten to the specified torque, and where locking washers are fitted fold up the edge of the washer so that it contacts the bolt head.

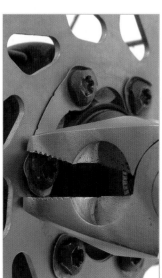

5 Shimano six-bolt rotors are often supplied with lock washers. Fully tighten the torx-headed bolts and then use a pair of pliers or a screwdriver to bend over the lock washer.

REPLACING THE BRAKE HOSE

If you need to replace the hydraulic brake hose then the replacement hose must be cut squarely to the correct length. Each manufacturer has its own unique arrangement of hose end fittings. Some feature a crimped-on banjo-style fitting, but most use a gland nut and compressible olives. You will, of course, need to bleed the brakes after fitting a new hose. With the hose fitted and the system bled, apply the brakes and check closely for any leaks at the new fittings. It's a good idea to take the bike on a short test ride and then recheck the security of the fittings on your return.

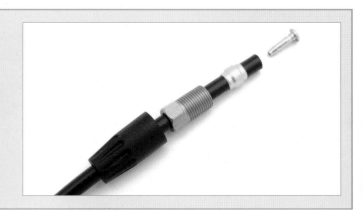

Changing hydraulic disc brake pads

1 Having removed the appropriate wheel, use a pair of pliers to close the end of the split pin.

2 Pull out and discard the split pin. On some designs the brake pads may well fall out of the bottom of the caliper at this point.

3 Remove the spring clip and then pull out the worn brake pads.

4 The pistons must now be pushed back into the caliper body. Special tools are available for this task, but on this particular caliper a spanner works well.

5 An alternative method is to push the piston back into the caliper using a pair of combination pliers. Take care not to damage the piston face or mark the caliper body.

6 Assemble the new pads and spring retainer and slide them into the caliper. Fit a new split pin and splay the end of the pin open. With the wheel and disc rotor fitted OR holding a loose rotor between the pads, work the brake lever a few times to check the operation.

DISC BRAKE PADS

Some of the many shapes and sizes of disc brake pads on the market today. The most common braking materials are often described as 'organic' or 'sintered'. Ceramic and Kevlar pads are also available.

Most pads have a 2 or 3mm braking surface bonded to a metal backing plate. These pads have all been used. Some are worn at the edges; on others the braking surface is starting to crack, while yet others are still serviceable.

WHEN YOU NEED TO DO THIS:
- When the brake pads are worn.
- Bleed and replace the brake fluid when the brakes feel spongy or the fluid in the reservoir becomes discoloured.

TIME:
- Allow an hour for a simple brake-pad change. Bleeding the brakes can easily take an hour per brake.

DIFFICULTY: 🔧🔧🔧🔧
- Brake pads are fairly simple to change, but bleeding brakes can sometimes be very problematic.

BMX brakes

You'll find a variety of brake systems fitted to BMX bikes. The most commonly fitted type are referred to as U brakes, which are similar in operation to cantilever brakes. Scaled-down V brakes are also sometimes fitted, as are side-pull brakes. On most U brakes the balance of the brake is adjusted by altering the tensioner return spring, normally via a lock nut and hex key. The rear brake is often fitted on the chain stays and features a straddle wire to bypass the seat post tube.

Perhaps the most unique feature of BMX brakes is their use of a brake cable detangler, often referred to as a 'gyro'. This is a system that allows a full 360° revolution of the handlebars to be performed without tangling up the cable for the rear brakes. The front brake employs a similar idea, with the brake cable travelling directly through the fork steerer and head tube. Adjustment is the same as most other brakes, but the important thing is to ensure that the movable collar at the head tube is balanced and parallel to the upper collar.

It's important to note that BMX bikes often lack their front brake. Whilst this may add a certain amount of street credibility, it's illegal to ride on a road in the UK without both a rear brake and a front brake in good working order.

Adjusting BMX brakes

1 A noodle is often fitted to the front brakes. This is similar to the noodle fitted to V brakes. Check that this is free to move, removing it and lubricating it if necessary. If the front brake cable runs through the steerer, you'll find a very tight loop of cable and a cable guide on the front fork. Remove the cable from the brake and thoroughly lubricate it.

2 At the rear, unhook the brake cable from the brake-operating arm. Check that the brake arms move freely, adjusting and lubricating as necessary. With the cable unhooked, lubricate the inner cable.

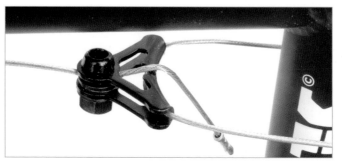

3 Tension the main cable and adjust the straddle wire cable so that it doesn't foul the seat post. Operate the brake and make sure that both arms of the caliper move equally. You may need to adjust the tension on each individual arm to achieve this. On most BMX brakes the tension is adjusted by undoing the lock nut and then rotating the hex-headed bolt in the correct direction.

4 Most gyro-type brake systems offer four points of adjustment at the head tube. The important point is to adjust the cables so that the fixed and movable parts of the gyro are parallel to each other.

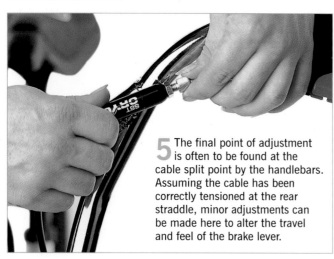

5 The final point of adjustment is often to be found at the cable split point by the handlebars. Assuming the cable has been correctly tensioned at the rear straddle, minor adjustments can be made here to alter the travel and feel of the brake lever.

WHEN YOU NEED TO DO THIS:
■ Whenever the brakes become hard to operate.

TIME:
■ Allow 30 minutes to lubricate and adjust the brakes.

DIFFICULTY: 🔧🔧🔧
■ There are a lot of adjustment points on BMX brakes. Work methodically and the job will be a lot easier.

Hub brakes

Hub brakes are less popular than they used to be, but are still fitted to top-of-the-range city and commuter bikes. They're often incorporated into a hub gear system and, where fitted to the front hub, they may also incorporate a dynamo-driven lighting system. Most are conventional drum-type brakes, where two brake shoes are forced against a drum. This is exactly the same system as fitted to motor vehicles except that they're cable-operated rather than hydraulically operated.

Shimano's roller brake is similar in operation to a drum brake, except that a series of rollers and cams force the brake shoes against the internal braking surface of the hub. Both systems are efficient and low-maintenance, hence their popularity on city bikes – occasional checking of the brake cable and the security of the hub fixings is usually all that's required.

Brake cable adjustment is carried out at the hub. Release the locking nut and turn the adjuster anticlockwise until the drum brake locks up. Now turn the adjuster clockwise until the hub rotates freely. Settle the brake by pulling on the brake lever a few times. Check that the wheel still rotates freely and then tighten the lock nut.

Shimano roller hub brake

1 To remove the wheel unhook the brake cable end.

2 This front hub brake has a dynamo fitted. Disconnect the electrical connector before slackening off the hub nuts.

3 Pull the wheel free of the fork. When refitting the reaction arm must be carefully guided into position.

4 It's possible to apply a small amount of grease to the inside of the roller brake occasionally.

CHAPTER

DRIVETRAIN

Components

For many years the bike drivetrain was a relatively simple affair. Bikes were single-speed or had three-speed internal hub gears. Racing bikes had a five- or six-speed friction shift derailleur gear system. Bottom brackets were adjustable and the cranks were held in place with cotter pins. Rear sprockets were threaded on to the rear hub and chains were $1/8$in or $3/32$in. Most components were compatible with other manufacturers' parts, and could be mixed and matched to suit your bike and your budget.

The advent of the mountain bike, modern production methods, the onward march of technology and Far Eastern mass production led to a massive change in components and the rise of new standards. Shimano has led the way with many innovations, including indexed gear-changing and 'freehub' cassettes.

Gear numbers have increased from 12-speed (a double chainring and a six-sprocket rear block) to 30-speed (a triple chainring and 10-speed cassette). In fact, 11-speed cassettes are also now available for road bikes. Not only do we have an increased number of gears, but we have more gear ratios to choose from. Hub gears have also seen a revival in recent years, progressing from the original three-speed hubs of Sturmey-Archer and other manufacturers to the 14-speed hubs available from Rohloff.

Many bottom brackets are now sealed with no adjustment possible or feature external bottom brackets. This development has gone hand in hand with the change from cotter pin cranks through square taper cranks to several versions of splined cranks on mid- to top-of-the-range bikes.

For the home mechanic, all these changes mean that it's important to know what systems are fitted to your bike. Before ordering any replacement parts, make sure you've identified what type of drivetrain it has, and if you're upgrading a component, check if you need any special tools. For example, the change from an old-style cone-and-cup bottom bracket to a sealed bottom bracket is a worthwhile upgrade, but you'll need the correct tool to fit the replacement.

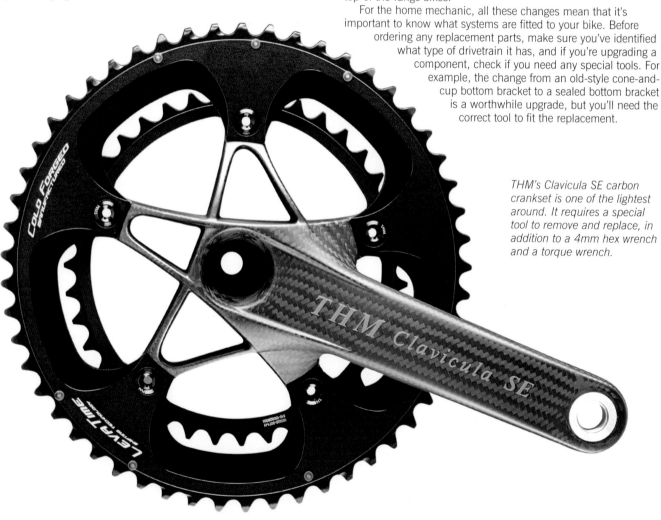

THM's Clavicula SE carbon crankset is one of the lightest around. It requires a special tool to remove and replace, in addition to a 4mm hex wrench and a torque wrench.

Drivechain components

1 This is a ³/₃₂in chain, suitable for up to eight-speed derailleur gears systems. Nine-, 10- and 11-speed chains are different widths.

2 Most single-speed bikes use a ¹/₈in chain, but some may have a ³/₃₂in chain fitted, so check carefully before buying a replacement.

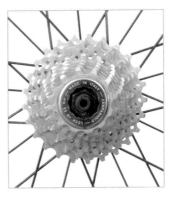

3 This is a cassette-style sprocket. It slides on to the 'freehub', which contains the ratchet that allows you to freewheel.

4 This is an old-style rear sprocket that screws on to the hub. The freewheel ratchet is part of the sprocket assembly.

5 Hub gears usually have a single sprocket that can be changed to make minor alterations to the gear ratio. Most use a ¹/₈in chain.

6 Fixie bikes have no freewheel system. You must pedal all the time. All track bikes have a fixed-wheel system.

7 Many rear derailleurs, like this one from SRAM, can be adjusted at the derailleur.

8 One-piece sealed bottom brackets are fitted to many bikes today. No adjustment is possible and they must be replaced as a complete unit.

9 A thin-wall socket or box spanner will be required to remove this type of crank-retaining bolt.

10 Recent developments have led to the external bottom bracket. The crank has more support as the bearings are now outside the BB shell.

Care and inspection

A clean, lubricated and correctly adjusted drivetrain is an efficient drivetrain. Dirt and muck on the chain acts as a very nice grinding paste, so follow the guidance on pages 40–41 and keep your chain clean and lubricated.

There is no hard and fast rule on replacing the chain. It will all depend on how often you ride, where you ride and the conditions you ride in. A chain on a mountain bike used off-road in the mud – especially if the local geology is a hard rock like granite – may only last a few hundred miles. A road bike that's never ridden in the rain may not need a new chain for several thousand miles. The best advice is to buy a chain-checking tool and use it to monitor the wear of the chain.

As the chain wears so do the chainrings and rear sprocket. However, the first moving parts to wear are often the jockey wheels on the rear derailleur. Next will be the most used sprocket on the cassette, so check these when you're checking the chain. Checking the wear on the rings and sprockets can be difficult. The wear can be easy to spot, but deciding if replacement is required is not so easy. If you've replaced the chain and are still having problems with the gears slipping and skipping, you'll need to replace the rest of the drivetrain components.

The classic sign of worn rings and sprockets is the development of a hooked profile on the teeth of the gears. On a mountain bike this can exhibit itself as the dreaded 'chain suck', when the small chainring – often called the 'granny ring' – won't let go and the chain wraps itself completely around it. The result is a complete lock-up of the drivetrain.

Don't overlook the security of the chainrings themselves. Most will use special chainring bolts to hold the rings in place, although cheaper cranksets will often have the rings riveted into place. Hold the crank arms and grab hold of each ring in turn to check that they're not loose. Whilst checking the rings it's also worth looking at and feeling the bottom bracket, which is often the source of many creaks and groans. If possible, drop off the chain, spin the cranks and listen for the rumble sound of worn bearings. Grab the cranks and feel for any play by pushing them in and out. A sealed bottom bracket will require replacement if any fault is found. An old-style cup and cone bottom bracket may be worth adjusting, but more often than not the best solution will be to upgrade to a sealed type.

At the rear, check the derailleur is secure. If your bike has a replaceable gear hanger, check that the bolts are tight. A quick alignment check should be carried out by sighting down the bike from the rear. Make sure the derailleur hangs vertically and that the jockey wheels are in good condition. Have a look at the rear cassette. Are the teeth worn or bent? Lift the rear wheel off the ground and pedal backwards. Listen for any unusual noises from the cassette freehub.

WHEN YOU NEED TO DO THIS:
- About every two or three months for a bike in regular use. For bikes used occasionally once a year should suffice.
- After any crash or accident when the bike has landed on its right (drive) side.

TIME:
- Fifteen minutes for a complete inspection.

DIFFICULTY: 🔧🔧
- It can be difficult to decide which part of a drivechain is causing a problem.

CHAIN LINE AND GEAR SELECTION
On a triple-chainring bike, select the middle ring and the middle sprocket at the rear. Turn the bike upside down and sight down the chain. The chain should be straight – more or less. If it's dramatically out then first check the frame for any obvious damage. Next check the bottom bracket – it's possible that the wrong one has been fitted, especially if the chainset seems to be too far out from the frame. If nothing seems obviously wrong, it may be wise to have the frame alignment checked.

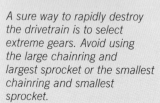

A sure way to rapidly destroy the drivetrain is to select extreme gears. Avoid using the large chainring and largest sprocket or the smallest chainring and smallest sprocket.

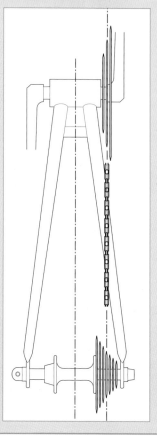

In an ideal world all chain lines would look like this 21-speed (3 x 7) system.

Drivetrain inspection

1 A crude but quick check is to lift the chain off the big chainring. Anything more than a slight movement requires investigation.

2 Check the security of the chainring mounting bolts. If any are loose you'll need a special screwdriver to tighten the sleeve nut at the rear.

3 A hooked profile is a sign of a worn chainring or sprocket. This chainring requires replacement along with a new chain and cassette. Never replace rings and sprockets without replacing the chain at the same time.

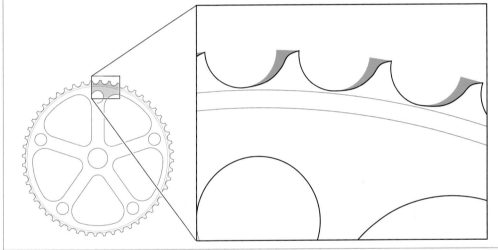

4 Grab hold of the cranks and attempt to rock them from side to side. Any movement should be investigated. First, check the tightness of the crank mounting bolts. If these are fine the play may well be in the bottom bracket.

5 With the chain off, give the cranks a spin in both directions. Listen for any creaks, groans or a rumbling sound – all signs of a worn bottom bracket.

6 Bent chainrings can be a common problem, so sight down the bike and watch the gap between the chainrings and chain stay as you rotate the crank. A bent ring will be easily spotted.

Cleaning and checking chains

In many ways the adoption of a chain-drive system was the foundation of the modern bicycle. Up to this point all early bicycles were single-speed, direct drive machines. The use of a chain allowed rear-wheel drive, gear system development and front-wheel steering. The distance between each link on a bicycle chain is common to all chains at ½in from the centre of one roller pin to the next. However, the width varies with each application.

Single-speed and most hub-geared bikes use a ⅛in chain width and derailleur-geared bikes traditionally used ³/₃₂in. The introduction of nine-, 10- and 11-speed gear systems has led to a further narrowing of chain widths to accommodate more closely spaced sprockets in the same space on the rear hub. There is no standard for chain widths and consequently there are minor variations between manufacturers for the same drive system. For example, Shimano nine-speed chains are 6.6mm wide and Sram nine-speed chains are 6.9mm. This isn't normally a problem, since both chains are sold as 'nine-speed compatible' and are interchangeable.

Chain-drive is a very efficient method of converting your leg power into forward momentum. A clean chain in good condition will maximise efficiency. We've covered chain cleaning in Chapter 2, but for a more thorough job the chain is best removed from the bike and soaked in a suitable solvent. This is easy to do on chains fitted with a quick link connector like Sram's 'Powerlink', but if you have a Shimano chain you'll need a new connector pin.

No matter how meticulous you are with chain cleaning, it will eventually wear out and require replacement. Chains don't stretch – a common misconception – but the distance between the pins increases due to wear, mostly on the pins and rollers. A worn chain will quickly start to wear the sprockets and chainrings. If the chain is replaced before it becomes excessively worn, then new sprockets and chainrings won't be needed. However, the chain can only be replaced

a certain number of times before the sprockets and chainrings will require replacement too.

All the major component makers (Sram, Shimano and Campagnolo) supply their own brand of chains. Quality chains are also available from Connex and KMC, amongst others. In addition each manufacturer offers different quality chains, with different prices to match.

CLEANING FLUIDS
Chain-cleaning machines will often be supplied with a suitable cleaning agent. Once this has been used up it's best replaced with a similar product. Don't be tempted to use an aggressive solvent as it may attack the machine's plastic components. Stick to a biodegradable solvent where possible and dispose of the contaminated fluid sensibly. If you remove the chain for cleaning, an old biscuit tin makes a suitable container. Use a proprietary degreasing solvent and not a home-brewed cocktail. Again, dispose of the contaminated fluid in a sensible manner.

Easy chain cleaning

1 Always take the worst of the grime and dirt off first with a hose or brush and a bucket of water.

2 The edge of a cloth can be used to clean between the sprockets, but a special cassette cleaning brush will make the job a lot easier. These aren't very expensive.

3 Use a cleaning fluid and an old toothbrush on the chain rollers. Place a tray under the chain to catch the excess.

4 Use a water dispersing spray such as WD40 or GT85 to drive out the moisture. Dry off the chain and lubricate with your preferred chain lube.

Checking chain wear

1 The traditional method of checking the chain was with a steel ruler. However, most of the wear on a chain is on the rollers.

2 A new chain should measure exactly 12in over 12 complete links, from centre to centre of the roller pins.

3 A far more effective method is to use one of the chain-checking tools now available. This is a seriously worn chain that requires immediate replacement.

4 The checking tool in use on a brand-new chain.

WHEN YOU NEED TO DO THIS:
■ For a bike in regular use every two months or so. For off-road mountain bikes after every ride.

TIME:
■ Fifteen minutes for a complete clean and lube.

DIFFICULTY:
■ A straightforward and simple job.

CHAIN PARTS

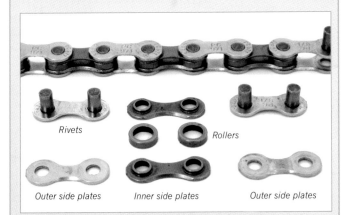

Rivets   *Rollers*

Outer side plates   *Inner side plates*   *Outer side plates*

Chains are made out of several component parts. This is a good quality nine-speed chain suitable for most bikes. Better-quality chains may also have rubber O-rings fitted alongside the inner rollers.

WHAT CHAIN?

The make of chain fitted can often be seen on the side plate. Clean the chain and check if you're looking at a like-for-like replacement.

Shimano chains are marked 'UG', 'IG' or 'HG'; Campagnolo chains have a 'C' mark; and Sram chains are often marked with 'PC' followed by two or three numbers to indicate the model and type.

Removing and replacing chains

A worn chain needs replacing. Clean the chain and check it as described on pages 76–77. Next you'll need to identify the chain and how the ends are joined: ⅛in chains, as fitted to single-speed bikes, normally have a horseshoe spring clip joining links; Shimano chains are joined with a special pin and can be split at any point; and Sram chains (and other makes) have a special quick-release connecting link that's often a different colour to the chain, which makes locating it somewhat easier. Some chains don't have a special link and can be split at any point.

You'll need a chain-splitting tool if you're replacing the chain or have one without a removable link, and you need a special tool to remove Shimano chains. It should also be noted that some manufacturers don't recommend reusing the removable link. This appears to only be applicable to 10-speed chains, so check with the manufacturer to see if their link is reusable.

INNER LINK

OUTER LINK

CONNECTING PIN

STIFF LINKS

Occasionally you will come across a stiff link in the chain. The usual cause is poor maintenance or the chain has been damaged by mangled gear changes. It will often be felt as the stiff link passes around the rear derailleur jockey wheels. This is the best place to spot it, with the bike on a stand or placed upside down.

It can often be freed by gently flexing the chain between your hands. Alternatively, the chain splitting tool can be used to apply a little pressure to the stiff link.

Shimano chain tool

REPLACEMENT RIVET

HANDLE

GUIDES

PUNCH

Removing standard chains

1 Wind out the pin and place the chain on the front guides. The Shimano chain tool can be used if required – just adjust the back support so that it rests on the back of the chain.

2 Gradually wind the pin in so that it's centred on the centre of the rivet head. Screw fully home – about six turns. Most quality chain tools are designed to stop before the pin has been pushed fully out.

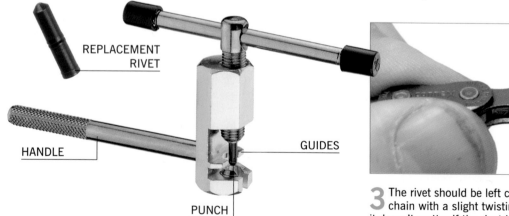

3 The rivet should be left captive in the outer plate. Separate the chain with a slight twisting action. If you're replacing the chain, it doesn't matter if the rivet is pushed fully out.

Removing Shimano chains

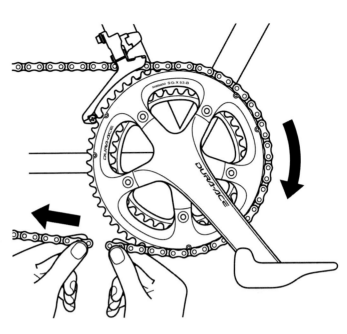

1 Never split a Shimano chain at a black rivet – always choose a silver one. Adjust the back screw so that it firmly supports the chain. Wind in the tool and centre it on the pin.

2 A fair amount of force is required to push out the rivet. Continue screwing in the pin until the rivet falls out.

SHIMANO CHAINS
Shimano replacement pins come as a black pin for seven- and eight-speed systems; a silver pin for nine-speed systems; a silver pin with double lines marked on the end for 10-speed systems; and a silver pin with a slightly more pointed end for 11-speed. Always use the correct pin and always remove the rivet from the leading edge of the chain as shown here.

3 To join the chain slide in a new rivet and then fit the chain into the chain tool. Screw in the pin so that it meets the new rivet in the centre.

4 Keep screwing in the chain tool pin until the break-off point emerges on the far side of the chain. Use a pair of pliers to snap off the end of the new rivet.

Removing quick-link chains

1 The 'Powerlink' is Sram's version of a quick-link. Conveniently it's a gold colour so that you can locate it easily.

2 Hold the links either side of the Powerlink and push together. Note: this can be tough and might require pliers.

3 The link will slide together, ready to be separated.

4 The side plates are now separated. Check for any damage, especially where the rivet head sits in the closed position. Reverse the procedure to refit the link.

Removing a ⅛in chain with a master link

1 On bikes fitted with chain guards, it's always easier to remove the chain if you take the guard off first.

2 Locate the master link by turning the cranks. Use a stubby screwdriver to pry the spring free.

3 With the retaining clip removed, the link can be separated.

4 When refitting the chain, the closed end of the spring clip must point forward in the direction of travel.

Fitting a new chain

New chains are always supplied with more links than you'll need. The average is around 114 links, and the majority of bikes require around 110. These are, of course, very average figures. The simplest way to decide on a new chain length is to compare it with the old one. On a clean surface place the old chain next to the new and line them up side by side. Remove the excess links with a chain tool.

The standard method recommended by most chain manufacturers is to wrap the chain around the large chain wheel at the front and the largest sprocket at the rear. Don't thread it through the derailleur at this point. Bring the ends tightly together and then add two complete links. This method works well for all rigid bikes with a derailleur gear system.

On bikes with rear suspension, if you don't have the old chain for comparison or you aren't happy with the gear change, then you'll need to remove the rear spring (or let the air out of an air shock) and fully compress the suspension to work out the point at which chain growth is at its maximum. On many rear-suspension designs this will be at or near full travel. If you have an old URT (unified rear triangle) suspension design, where the bottom bracket is part of the swing arm, you can use the method outlined for a rigid bike because there's no chain growth on URT bikes.

On single-speed bikes the position of the rear wheel in the horizontal dropouts must be considered. If the chain is fitted with the wheel fully forward you won't be able to unhook the chain to remove the wheel; too far back and you may not be able to tension the chain correctly. We examine the intricacies of single-speed chains in more depth on page 82.

SPECIAL PINS ATTACHMENT

Campagnolo chain installation

Campagnolo's 10-speed and 11-speed chains use a special replacement pin, which comprises two parts: the pin and the pilot. Engage the pilot and pin so that the pin faces the inside of the bike and the pilot is inside the link. The pin is then pushed outward, away from the spokes until it's fully inserted in the link.

Campagnolo makes a special tool (pictured) for installing 10-speed and 11-speed chains. If you don't have this tool, it's especially important to press down on the chain at the pin to keep it seated in the chain tool. Use your thumb to hold the link in place as you insert it. After the pin is fully inserted, simply pull outward to remove the pilot.

Shimano chain installation

Align the ends of the chain and insert the special replacement pin into the holes, tapered end first. Now place the chain tool on the chain so that the link you're working on is seated completely and resting against the back shelf of the tool. Drive the replacement pin into the chain – this will push the pilot part of the pin out the other side. To finish installing the pin, break off the pilot, which will snap off if you grab it with pliers and bend. On some chain tools, you can also slip it into the head of the tool and twist to snap it off.

1 Wrap the new chain around the large chainring and largest sprocket. Pull it tight. Note where the two ends overlap and add two links.

REPAIRING A BENT CHAIN

If you notice an intermittent skipping as you pedal, you might have a bent or twisted portion of your chain. This is relatively common and can happen if, for example, a twig is drawn into your drivetrain and you continue to pedal.

To fix the problem, back-pedal with your hand and carefully observe the path of the chain. Watch ever so closely for 'bad links' passing through the jockey wheels of the rear derailleur. If they're badly bent, they will really stand out.

Once isolated, pull back on the chain so that you can hold the chain either side of the bad link. Now you simply twist, using your hands or, more likely, pliers. It sounds a little crude but with a bit of effort and trial and error, you'll straighten out the bent section enough to ride home. When home, it's a wise idea to replace the damaged links because their integrity would have been threatened.

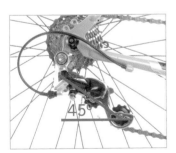

2 Use the chain link breaker tool to remove the excess links.

3 Thread the chain through the rear derailleur and join the ends together with the special pin (Shimano and Campagnolo chains) or the quick link connector.

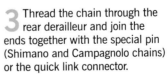

4 Cycle through the gears and check the derailleur position in the lowest gear. At this point there should still be some movement available at the rear mech. The derailleur will be at approximately 45° to the ground.

5 Now move the chain to the highest gear. An imaginary line drawn through the centre of the derailleur jockey wheels will be at 90° to the ground – more or less – if the chain is the correct length.

WHEN YOU NEED TO DO THIS:
■ When the chain is worn.

TIME:
■ Allow 15 minutes to change a chain fitted with a quick-link connector. Allow another ten minutes or so for dealing with Shimano chains.

DIFFICULTY: ✐✐✐
■ Fairly straightforward with a quality chain link tool.

Single-speed chain

The 2000s saw the rise of fixed-gear and single-speed bikes. They tailed off slightly but have enjoyed a second wind thanks to bikes from the likes of Mango, Charge and Brick Lane Bikes. As the name suggests, single-speed bikes are just that – they have a sole single gear. Fixed-gear are the same but, as we mentioned earlier in this guide, you can't freewheel. Many bikes have the option of flipping the hub of the wheel to change between single-speed and fixed-gear.

The lack of derailleur and gears may require more physical effort but it also means these popular bikes are easier to maintain. But not as easy as you'd think. Achieving the correct chain tension for proficient pedalling can be achieved via a top-end eccentric bottom bracket. However, most single-speeds don't come with these; instead, you can achieve ideal chain tension with what's called a 'chain tug', which you can pick up for as little as £2…

1 To judge whether your chain's at optimum tension is easy – simply apply forefinger pressure at the base of the chain.

2 In the case of this bike, the chain is slack and needs fine-tuning.

3 Firstly, undo the axle nut with the correct-sized spanner. In this case, it's a 15mm socket on a ratchet.

4 Remove the nut from the axle and put it somewhere safe.

5 Place the chain tug over the rear axle and rear of the chainstays.

6 Tighten the chain-tug nut by hand, just to keep it in place. The nut should sit flush against the horizontal dropouts.

7 Bring back the wheel nut to the bike's axle and tighten by hand.

8 Using a spanner or socket, tighten the chain-tug nut. At the same time, pull the wheel backwards and tension the chain. (You can also add a chain tug to the non-driveside.)

9 When you're happy with chain tension – 12mm chain travel when pushed downward between front and rear sprockets – tighten the wheel nut.

10 Look down and check the wheel is straight in the dropouts. You have to balance the left and right tensions of the two chain tugs.

11 With the wheel centred, torque the wheel nuts to the manufacturer's specified torque settings.

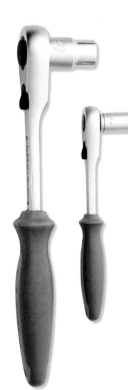

TOOLS NEEDED
Apart from two chain tugs – you can use one but two are recommended – the only tools you need are spanners, ideally on a ratchet for greater purchase. Axle nuts generally require a 15mm spanner; the other is dependent on chain-tug size. Ours was 10mm.

WITHOUT A CHAIN TUG

If you don't have access to a chain tug, don't despair. Simply follow this procedure instead... Position the wheel squarely in the dropouts, about 10mm or so from their front end. Wrap the chain around both sprockets and pull it tight. Remove the excess links and join the chain together.

Now adjust the chain tension by moving the wheel back in the dropouts so that there's approximately 10 to 15mm of slack in the centre of the top of the chain. Rotate the cranks and check the tension in several positions, as slightly oval chainrings are common. You may have to compromise the tension if this is the case. Use a ruler if necessary to check that the rear wheel is correctly aligned between the chain stays and then tighten the wheel nuts.

When the tension is correct, check and if necessary adjust the brakes. This is especially important on BMX bikes where the brake is fitted to the chain stays.

Some high-end bikes (and the primary chain on tandems) may have an eccentric bottom bracket fitted. On these bikes it's possible to rotate the bottom bracket to take up the slack in the chain. Some may require special tools, but most can be adjusted with hex keys and a peg-type spanner.

Fitting new gear cables

It's a false economy not to replace gear cables with top-quality ones. Even the best cables are inexpensive. Most are 1.1 or 1.2mm diameter stainless steel cables, and the end fittings are universal. Teflon-coated cables are available, but these should only be used if you're fitting new outer cables at the same time.

Gear cable outers are nominally 4mm in diameter, but this will vary slightly from manufacturer to manufacturer. Unlike brake cables that are spiral wound, gear cable outers have the wire strands running parallel along the cable. This makes them difficult to cut, so a quality pair of cable cutters is essential. All cables require new end-caps to be fitted.

If you're replacing both the inner and outer cables on a bike that sees regular use, it may be worthwhile upgrading the cable to a sealed cable

set. These often have Teflon-coated inners and Teflon-lined outers. Don't lubricate these cables as Teflon is the lubricant. Special seals designed to minimise water penetration are often provided in these sets. When replacing cables, always use the old cable outer as a template for cutting the new one. If you've changed the rear derailleur, check the new cable runs closely, as newer derailleurs often have a changed location for the outer cable.

New cables take a while to settle down. Before cutting the inner cable, it's worth pulling hard on it with a pair of pliers. Fit the cable into the derailleur and move the gear changer to the position where the inner cable is under the most tension. This will be on the largest sprocket at the rear on 'normal' derailleurs and on the biggest chainring at the front. Leave the cables under tension for as long as possible before adjusting the indexing.

Flat-bar bikes

1 Move the gears to the position where the cable is at its slackest. Remove the cable cover screw. These are usually plastic and are easily lost. On some set-ups you may have to move the brake or the gear changer to access the cable cover screw.

2 Loosen the clamp bolt at the derailleur (or cut the cable) and then pull down the outer cable. Push the inner cable out of the gear shifter. If you have difficulty, make sure the correct gear has been selected. The head of the cable is normally visible through the access hole.

3 On some bar-mounted shifters you may have to remove the lower cover to remove the cable. Take care not to lose the small screws.

4 On Shimano 'RevoShift' gear changers you'll have to remove the gear indicator cover first to access the cable. This is held in place by two very small crosshead screws – don't lose them.

5 With the cover removed, pull out the inner gear cable. If you have trouble, it can sometimes be pushed out or released with a pair of needle-nose pliers.

6 On Gripshift gear changers you'll have to remove the handlebar grips first. With the Gripshift removed, rotating the shifter allows the movable collar to be pulled free. The gear cable can then be accessed and removed.

Combined brake and gear levers

Shimano, Campagnolo and Sram produce a combined system for road bikes with drop handlebars. For the racing cyclist, these systems have the major advantage that you don't need to take your hands off the handlebars to change gear, unlike the traditional down-tube-mounted gear changer.

To replace the inner cables on all the systems shown here, always engage the highest gear – the cable will be under little or no tension. Release the cable clamp nut or bolt at the derailleur and remove the cable end crimp.

Newer systems have both the gear and brake cables routed beneath the handlebar tape, and so to replace the outer cables new bar tape will be required. However, because the cables are hidden under the tape and are high up and away from all the road dirt, this should be a fairly infrequent job. If you're replacing the bar tape because it's worn out or damaged, it will be worth removing and checking the cable outers at the very least.

Shimano STi levers

1 On the Shimano system, the gear cable emerges from the side. The brake is the large lever – as it is on all the systems shown here.

2 The brake cable is pulled out from the front. Pull the brake lever down to access the cable.

   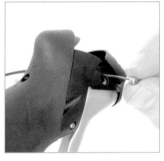

3 Hold the brake lever open with a tie wrap and feed in the new cable.

4 To change the gear cable inner, hold the lever back with a tie wrap or cord. Note the groove in the side for the lever clamp fitting bolt.

5 A small rubber bung covers the gear cable access hole. If you can't see the cable end fitting, change gear until it becomes visible.

6 Push the cable up from the down tube and pull it free. Fit the new cable in reverse order.

Campagnolo 'Ergopower' levers

 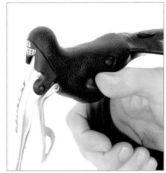  

1 This is Campagnolo's 'Veloce' ('rapid' or 'quick' in English) combined brake and gear lever.

2 The Campagnolo mechanism is in the body of the lever and consequently has a longer body.

3 Peel back the hood from the lever body, working it over the small lever as you go.

4 Working from the opposite side, push the cable up from where it's exposed at the down tube and hook it free with a small screwdriver if necessary.

Sram 'DoubleTap' levers

1 The Sram 'DoubleTap' system is very sleek, with all the gear change functions in one lever.

2 To replace the brake cable, pull the brake on and push up the inner from an exposed section on the top tube.

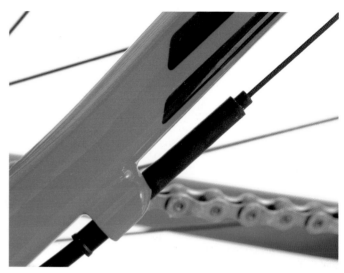

CABLE SEALS
Various cable seals are available to help minimise water penetration. They're a useful addition to any exposed inner cables, as seen here on this seat-stay cable stop.

3 The gear cable is accessed by peeling back the lever hood. Push the gear cable inner up from an exposed section on the down tube.

4 The cable will emerge from the inside of the lever. Fit a new one and fold the hood back into position.

CABLE CRIMPS
A cable crimp should always be fitted to the cable end to stop the cable from fraying. If you don't have a crimp, wipe the cable free of any lube and apply a small drop of superglue.

WHEN YOU NEED TO DO THIS:
- When gear selection becomes problematic.
- If the cable is frayed.

TIME:
- Allow 20 minutes per cable. Road testing and final adjustment can quite easily add another 30 minutes.

DIFFICULTY: 🔧🔧🔧
- A simple cable change is straightforward. Things can get complicated if you need to replace the outer cables, especially on road bikes with drop handlebars.

SPECIAL CABLE SET
Complete specialist cable sets are available. These have more than enough outer cable for most applications. They're supplied complete with end fittings and cable crimps. However, it's sometimes more cost-effective to simply buy the cable outer by the metre. You will, of course, also need cable end fittings and some cable crimps. These items can often be worth buying in bulk (at a reduced price, of course) if you have several bikes to maintain and repair.

Internal gear cables

Like internal brake routing, which we covered on page 57, internal gear cable routing is appearing on an increasing number of bikes, particularly those at the top end of the market. Again, they're designed to not only make your pride and joy look less cluttered, but by shielding things from the outside, you not only add longevity to the parts but also improve your bike's aerodynamic profile.

In this step-by-step, we show you how to remove and replace internal gear cables. We focus heavily on the removal of the gear cable and fitting of the temporary plastic tubing. This tubing ensures you can guide the old cable out and new cable in seamlessly. However, if you try without plastic tubing and can't guide your inner cable to the exit holes, a magnet helps.

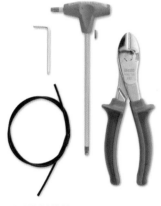

TOOLS NEEDED
For this job you'll need s internal brake cable routing, namely cable cutters, plastic tubing, and 2mm and 4mm or 5mm Allen keys.

1 Remove the gear cable from the rear derailleur. In general, this requires a 4mm or 5mm Allen key.

2 Unhook the cable from any external guides to relieve tension in the cable.

3 Unscrew the grub screw where the cable exits the top tube. Remove the outer cable and leave aside.

4 You might have to do similar at the bottom-bracket end and also the chainstays. Or it might simply be plastic ferrules placed in the holes in the frame.

5 With thin plastic tubing (black here but often transparent) long enough to reach through the frame, slide over the existing inner gear cable.

6 Slide the plastic tubing all the way through the frame. You can tape it to the frame to avoid pulling it out as you now pull the inner gear cable through the tubing. Guide new inner back through tubing.

7 Once inner gear cable's through, refit outer cable – which is housed externally – and connect to lever. Then remove plastic thin tubing from near the bottom bracket and complete fit at rear.

Adjusting derailleur gears

Before attempting any adjustment to either the front or rear derailleurs, it's essential that the drivetrain is in good condition. Check the condition of the gear cables (see pages 84–85) and the chainrings and rear cassette (pages 74–77). Next have a look at the rear and front derailleurs. The rear should hang more or less vertically when viewed from the back of the bike. It shouldn't be twisted or have excessive play in any of the pivots. The front mech should be correctly positioned as described on pages 90–91.

Most bikes will have an indexed gear system fitted, either operated by a handlebar-mounted gear changer or, on older road bikes, a down-tube-mounted gear changer. Older bikes will have a 'friction' shift system, where you manually choose the gear lever position and fine-tune it so that the gears are fully engaged. All gear changers are commonly referred to as 'shifters'.

All derailleurs have two small adjustment screws fitted. These are marked 'H' for high and 'L' for low. They're used to set the upper and lower limits of the derailleur's travel. Without them the chain and derailleur could drop into the spokes or off the small sprocket and into the drop out. On the front derailleur they stop the chain dropping on to the bottom bracket shell at one end and over the top of the big chainring at the other.

Rear derailleur adjustment

Before any adjustment can be made, it will be necessary to check the alignment of the rear derailleur. It should hang vertically below the cassette sprockets and should not be twisted. This can be done by eye or with greater accuracy using an alignment tool.

The derailleur high and low stops must be checked and adjusted before the gear cable. To adjust the rear stops, first loosen and pull free the gear cable. To make setting easier you could remove the chain, though this isn't essential. First adjust the 'H' stop. This stop is for the smallest sprocket at the rear, and is where the derailleur will naturally sit. Adjust the stop screw until the upper jockey wheel is directly below the outside edge smallest sprocket.

Next the 'L' stop screw requires setting. If the chain has been removed, pull the rear mech backwards and push it up to the large sprocket. With a little practice you'll feel the mech hitting the upper stop screw as you move it across. Hold the mech against the stop screw and check that it's directly below the large sprocket. Adjust the 'L' stop screw if necessary. If the chain is on the bike you'll have to hand-crank the pedals round while pushing the mech up to the low gear position.

Let the mech drop down – or wind the cranks round – to the smallest sprocket. With the shifter in the high gear position, pull the gear cable tight and tighten up the cable clamp bolt. Refit the chain if you removed it and select the middle ring if a triple chainset is fitted. On a road-bike double chainset, select the smaller front chainring. Use the shifter and cycle up and down the gears a few times, finishing in high gear. Check the cable tension. If the cable is too slack, the chain will not change from a smaller sprocket to its larger neighbour when the shifter is moved. In this case, turn the barrel adjusters outwards to increase the cable tension. If the cable is too tight, the chain will move quickly to a larger sprocket but will be reluctant to change downward to a smaller sprocket. In this case, reduce the cable tension by screwing the barrel adjuster inwards. If the cable is really slack, wind in all the adjuster and reset the cable by slackening the clamp bolt and pulling through the slack cable. Tighten the bolt.

With a bit of luck the indexing will be now correct. Check it by selecting the middle sprocket with the shifter and looking (and listening) at the position of the chain. It should be sat in the middle of the sprocket and not rubbing against the adjacent sprockets. Fine-tune the barrel adjuster to achieve this position. Work the chain up and down the gears a few times and recheck the indexing. Road-test it next and then more fine-tuning may be required.

ELECTRONIC GROUPSET

Possibly the most significant innovation in recent times is the electronic groupset. A traditional, mechanical groupset utilises a cable to change gears when you click the integrated lever beside your brakes. The electronic groupset dispenses with this cable and features a wire, while instead of a gear lever you simply have buttons, which you press to activate the electronic gear shift on your rear cassette or upfront. A battery sits near the bottom bracket or is inserted into the seat post. While Shimano's Di2 set the bar for wired electronic groupsets, in 2015 SRAM evolved the idea further, becoming the first manufacturer to mass-market a wireless electronic groupset. Known as the eTap, it's received plaudits from riders and the industry alike. And like the Di2, one battery charge should last around 1,000km. This is all well and good but what are the mooted benefits over the mechanical version? In no particular order, they are: more precise, quicker gear changes; reduced chainwear; automatic 'trim' function for the front derailleur; and the ability to make multiple shifts at one time. They're impressive but expensive, and you must remember to charge that battery.

1 There's little point in setting up the rear derailleur if the gear cables are in poor condition. Check them and lubricate them before you start. It's possible to set up the gears with the bike upside down, but the best solution is to suspend it in a bike stand.

2 Identify the 'H' (high) and 'L' (low) adjustment screws. These marks are often hard to see, so once you have identified them consider marking one with correction fluid or similar. Slacken off the gear cable and set up the high gear position of the mech. Use the 'H' screw to align the inside edge of the top jockey wheel with the outside edge of the smallest sprocket.

3 There are several ways to adjust the low gear stop. The easy way is to remove the chain and push the mech over. You can do this with the chain on if you wish, but you'll need to rotate the cranks as you do so. Alternatively, tighten the cable clamp and use the shifter to move to low gear. Adjust the 'L' screw so that the jockey wheel is directly below the largest sprocket.

MECH HANGER

All aluminium, carbon fibre and some steel frames will have a replaceable rear mech hanger fitted. This is designed to break off in the case of a crash. If it's bent or damaged it will require replacement. Many mountain bikers always carry a spare with them in their toolkit. Each bike has its own unique hanger, so it will always be worth ordering a spare from your local bike shop, even if you don't carry it with you on a bike ride.

4 Move the mech into the highest gear and tighten the gear cable. With the front mech in the middle ring (or the smaller ring on a double chainset), select the middle ring at the rear. Make small adjustments to cable tension with the barrel adjuster so that the chain runs smoothly over the sprocket. Run up and down the gears and adjust cable tension if necessary.

'H' AND 'L' LOCATION

At the back wheel:
- The small sprocket is the high gear; the stop screw is marked 'H'.
- The large sprocket is the low gear; the stop screw is marked 'L'.

At the pedals:
- The small chainring is the low gear; the stop screw is marked 'L'.
- The large chainring is the high gear; the stop screw is marked 'H'.

THE 'B' POST ADJUSTER

Most traditional rear mechs have a small screw for adjusting the tension in the main mounting pivot spring. This is the 'B' post or chain tension adjusting screw. Adjustment will be required if the top jockey wheel is too close to the large (low gear) sprocket. Move the front mech onto the small chainring and move the rear mech into low gear. Adjust the screw so that the jockey wheel clears the sprocket.

SRAM VS SHIMANO

Check before mixing Sram and Shimano components on a bike. Most parts are interchangeable, but not shifters and derailleurs. Sram list some shifters and derailleurs as Shimano-compatible, but most aren't. This is due to the amount of cable pull for each manufacturer's indexing system. SRAM use a 1:1 ratio, while Shimano and Campagnolo broadly use 1.7:1 and 1.5:1, respectively.

FRONT MECH

A huge range of front derailleurs are available. This is a modern top swing (the pivots are above the mounting band) dual-pull mountain bike front mech. The cable can enter from above or below. Various diameter clamp sizes are available, as well as 'braze-on' and 'E'-type derailleurs. Braze-on mechs have a screw fitting on the seat tube for the mech; 'E'-type mechs are clamped in place by the bottom bracket.

Front derailleur adjustment

The procedure for adjusting the front derailleur is similar to the rear. First make sure the height is correctly set. The outer cage should just clear the large chainring. The cage should also be perfectly parallel to the chainring. Move the shifter to the low gear position and slacken off the cable clamp nut. Locate the low gear stop screw (marked 'L'), and with the chain on the middle sprocket at the rear, adjust the stop screw so that the inner cage is just clear of the chain.

Pull the slack out of the gear cable and fully tighten the clamp bolt. Rotate the cranks and move the mech up to the large chainring. Adjust the 'H' (high) stop screw so that the chain is pushed on to the chainring, but not over. The shifter should be fully engaged in the high position at this point. Rotate the cranks and cycle up and down the front chainrings a few times to settle everything. On a triple chainring set-up, select the middle ring and cycle up and down the rear cassette a few times.

Move the shifter to select the lowest gear at the front and check the cable tension. Remove any slack with the barrel adjuster at the shifter and then run up and down the rear cassette a few times. As the chain swings across, watch for it catching the edge of the mech cage. Some minor adjustment of the 'L' stop screw may be necessary when the lowest gear is selected at the rear. Move the front mech to the large chainring and repeat the procedure.

If you have a triple ring set-up, move the shifter to the middle ring and run through the gears at the rear. Make sure the chain doesn't foul the mech cage as the chain swings from high to low gear at the rear. Some minor adjustment of the cable tension may be required.

1 Replacement Shimano front mechs are supplied with an alignment guide. If you're adjusting or refitting a front mech, set it up to clear the large chainring by between 1–2mm.

2 Check that the cage of the front mech is parallel with the chainrings before making any adjustment. The chain is omitted here for clarity. Slacken off the gear cable.

3 With the chain on the small ring, adjust the 'L' screw so that the inner edge of the cage just clears the chain. Rotate the cranks a few times to check that the small chainring isn't bent and catching the cage.

4 Lift the front mech up towards the largest chainring and then adjust the position of the 'H' limit screw. The mech's outer edge should clear the large chainring by a millimetre or so.

5 Now fit the gear cable, seating it correctly in the cable stops. Fit it around the cable clamp and tighten the clamp.

6 Cut the cable to length and fit a crimp. Next, move the shifter to the middle ring (on a triple chainring set-up) and move the rear mech up and down through the gears. Check that the chain clears the front mech cage in all gears. Some minor adjustment of the cable tension may be required.

FINE-TUNING THE INDEXING

In a perfect world, following the adjustment procedures shown here would result in perfect, silent gear changes every time. The real world is a different proposition. Worn components and an imperfect chain line can make adjustment of the indexing problematic. You may have to compromise the shifting at some point, especially on the extreme gears. Always aim to get the indexing perfect in the gear ratios you use the most. If you live in a hilly area, you may want to bias the indexing

towards the lower gears, so start by setting up the indexing in third or fourth rather than the middle sprocket – assuming you are running a nine-speed system. Likewise with the stop screws, especially the low gear stop. You may find you need to adjust this back a little to let the indexing at the shifter drop fully home after the shift down.

On the front derailleur on full-suspension mountain bikes, you may have to make fine adjustments to the position of the mech to compensate for the up and down movement of the swinging arm. Sometimes very small adjustments to the angle of the mech in relation to the chainrings will let the chain move with the rear suspension and not rub against the derailleur cage.

The other issue you may come across with a triple chainring set-up is dropping down from the middle ring to the small ring (the 'granny ring'). At this point you're relying on the spring tension in the front mech to pull the chain over on to the small chainring. A tired spring may be the issue, but the problem can often be overcome by moving into a low gear at the rear first before moving into the 'granny' at the front.

WHEN YOU NEED TO DO THIS:
■ Whenever you change the gear cable.
■ When the indexing or shifting quality deteriorates.

TIME:
■ Fifteen minutes for minor adjustments, especially if you have a bike-stand to keep the rear wheel off the ground.

DIFFICULTY: ʄʄʄ
■ Not a particularly difficult job, but patience will be required to get the indexing working absolutely perfectly on some bikes.

Derailleur removal, overhaul and refitting

Rear derailleur

Most rear derailleurs are attached directly to the mech hanger (often called the gear hanger), which is often part of the rear dropout, particularly on steel-frame bikes. Most non-steel bikes feature a removable gear hanger. Older bikes and those that use a non-indexed gear system tend to use a derailleur that fits directly into the dropout. These are often called 'bracket-fit' derailleurs.

If you're replacing the mech because it's worn out or has been damaged in a crash, then a like-for-like replacement is the simple option. If you decide to upgrade to a higher specification derailleur, then the most important aspect to consider is getting the same cage length. Various cage lengths are available, to suit various gear combinations. Some replacements will state the maximum rear sprocket size, others the total capacity, which is calculated by adding the difference from the smallest to the largest sprocket at the rear, to the difference between the smallest chainring to the largest at the front. So on a 10-speed, 12- to 25-cassette, coupled with a 39/52 double chainring, we have a 13-tooth difference at the front and the rear, giving a total capacity of 26.

To confuse things slightly, Shimano will often state the maximum rear sprocket size and the maximum front difference permitted for any particular rear mech.

Removal of the rear mech requires removal of the chain and the gear cable. On bikes with a bracket-type derailleur, the rear wheel must be removed first and the small locking plate loosened before the mech can be removed. On all other types, a hex key will be needed to remove the mech from the hanger.

With the mech removed it should be cleaned and inspected. The most common wear points are the jockey-wheel teeth, the pivots of the parallelogram and the 'B' post pivot point. Don't be too concerned with any side-to-side play in the jockey wheels. They're designed to float slightly to aid gear changing. The mech can be stripped down and the jockey wheels replaced. Most mechs will have a small 'C'

clip holding the main mounting bolt and the pivot spring in place. This can be removed and the pivot cleaned and checked.

However, if you have a cheap rear derailleur fitted, the individual parts may not be available. Even where parts are available it will often make more sense to replace the mech with a better-quality one.

Replacing the rear mech can be a problem, as the mounting bolt is captive in the mech. Take your time to align the bolt with the gear hanger. Start slowly and, if any excessive resistance is felt, stop and start again. If you cross-thread the gear hanger on bikes with replaceable hangers, a new one can be fitted; on bikes with the hanger as part of the dropout, all is not lost, as it's possible to re-tap the threads. If the threads are really damaged a specialist repairer can drill out the hanger and fit a new threaded sleeve for you.

JOCKEY WHEELS
Take time to inspect the condition of the jockey wheels. The jockey wheel on the left is seriously worn and requires replacement. The jockey wheel in the centre is worn but usable and the jockey wheel on the right is a new one. Before replacing the jockey wheels, check the pivots and other moving parts of the derailleur for wear, as replacing the entire derailleur may be more cost effective than replacing just the jockey wheels.

PIVOT BOLT
If you're fitting a replacement derailleur it's worth rescuing the pivot bolt from the old mech. This makes a great tool for checking and cleaning up the thread of the gear hanger.

1 Remove the chain and the gear cable. Support the mech and using a quality hex key remove the mounting bolt.

2 Clean the mech and inspect it for wear. If you're stripping the mech to clean it, keep the jockey wheels in order, as they're different.

Rear mech – exploded view

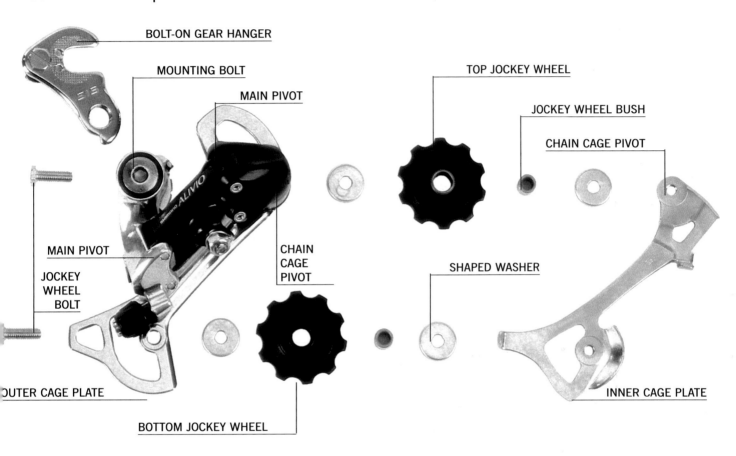

BOLT-ON GEAR HANGER

MOUNTING BOLT

MAIN PIVOT

TOP JOCKEY WHEEL

JOCKEY WHEEL BUSH

CHAIN CAGE PIVOT

MAIN PIVOT

JOCKEY WHEEL BOLT

CHAIN CAGE PIVOT

SHAPED WASHER

OUTER CAGE PLATE

INNER CAGE PLATE

BOTTOM JOCKEY WHEEL

3 Take care when refitting the mech. A finger placed behind the gear hanger will help guide the mech into place.

4 If you're just replacing the jockey wheels the chain can be left in position. Replace the jockey wheels one at a time.

5 Refit the mech, gear cable and chain. Adjust the indexing as described on pages 88–89.

Rear mech details

CAMPAGNOLO

With a long heritage in the manufacture of top-end road-bike components, Campagnolo produce derailleurs that should only be used in conjunction with a complete Campagnolo drivetrain.

SHIMANO

Shimano produce a vast range of rear derailleurs for all types of bike. The newer 'Shadow' rear mechs eliminate the large cable loop at the rear.

SRAM

Early Sram mechs were thermoplastic, newer ones are all-metal and the to-of-the-range mechs have carbon fibre cages. Only some are compatible with Shimano components, so check carefully if you're replacing Shimano or others with Sram.

MICROSHIFT

Microshift has been around since 1999 and is a small but growing company out of Taiwan. Their performance is comparable with models from the big three – Campag, Shimano and Sram – but generally come at a cheaper price point.

Front derailleur

Tucked away behind the front chainrings, the front derailleur doesn't suffer from the same wear issues as the rear. The major wear issue will mostly be confined to the pivot points and the inner edges of the cage. Take hold of the cage and see how much play there is in the pivot points by rocking it from side to side. It can be difficult assessing how much play is acceptable, but if you've been suffering from difficult gear changes and the mech cage is showing signs of wear then the derailleur may well be in need of replacement.

Just like the rear derailleur there are many types of front derailleur on the market. Traditional road bikes have a narrow-cage, bottom-pull, bottom-swing derailleur. Here the cable runs along the down tube, around the bottom bracket and up to the derailleur. It is bottom-swing because the mounting band is above the derailleur cage. The arrival of mountain bikes and the demands of touring cyclists led to the introduction of wide-cage mechs – to cope with triple chainrings – and top-swing, top-pull mechs to cope with interrupted seat tubes and full suspension.

Most front mechs are mounted to the seat tube with a simple clamping system and are supplied with shims to deal with the different-diameter seat tubes. Some road bikes will require a direct-mount derailleur to fit the brazed-on fitting on the seat tube. Shimano also supply an 'E'-type front mech that mounts to a special bracket that's held in place by the bottom bracket.

Realistically there are no serviceable parts on a front derailleur. If it's worn or damaged, replacement is the only option. If you're replacing the front mech, a like-for-like swap is the easy solution. If you decide to upgrade, the main consideration will be the seat tube diameter. The cable pull isn't such an issue, as many front derailleurs are dual-pull these days.

WHEN YOU NEED TO DO THIS:
■ When the derailleur is worn or damaged.

TIME:
■ Allow 15 minutes to replace a rear derailleur and at least 20 minutes to replace and set up the front derailleur.

DIFFICULTY: ///
■ Fairly straightforward to replace the rear derailleur, but the front derailleur often takes a little time to get just right.

1 Many front mechs have a cage that's screwed together. After removing the gear cable and the mounting clamp, the screw can be removed.

2 With care, gently prise apart the front mech cage and slip it off the chain. On front mechs with a riveted cage the chain must be removed.

3 Replacement Shimano front mechs are supplied with a stuck-on guide. If you're refitting the old mech, position it to give about 2mm clearance between the outer cage and the large chainring.

4 With the height set, rotate the mech so that it's parallel with the chainring.

5 Refit, or preferably replace, the gear cable. Make sure the shifter is in the low gear position, pull the inner cable tight and tighten the clamp bolt. Follow the adjustment procedure as shown on pages 90–91.

6 Braze-on road-bike front mechs can be removed in a similar manner to the clamp-on (or 'band on' as it's often called) derailleur.

7 Braze-on front mechs don't have any rotational adjustment. However, a small amount of vertical adjustment is often provided.

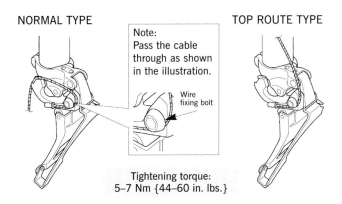

NORMAL TYPE   TOP ROUTE TYPE

Note:
Pass the cable through as shown in the illustration.

Wire fixing bolt

Tightening torque:
5–7 Nm {44–60 in. lbs.}

CABLE ROUTING
Many newer front derailleurs are dual-pull. They may be top-swing or bottom-swing, as shown here.

'E'-TYPE FRONT DERAILLEURS
To cope with the increasing variety of seat post angles, and on some suspension bikes the lack of a proper seat post, Shimano introduced a mounting plate for the front mech that's held in place by the bottom bracket.

Cassettes, blocks and sprockets

E ach individual gear at the rear is commonly called a sprocket, so a single-speed bike has a single sprocket. Derailleur gears that have multiple sprockets are often referred to as a 'rear block', 'rear cluster' or, more commonly today, a 'cassette'. The main difference is that cassette-type gears slide on to the rear hub and are held in place with a locking ring. Rear blocks are screwed onto the rear hub, as are most single-speed sprockets.

Screw-on blocks and sprockets have the freewheel ratchet as part of the assembly; cassette gears have the freewheel assembly as a separate item, mounted to the hub. This is now the most common system for derailleur-geared bikes. Shimano introduced the cassette system to enable the hub bearings to be moved to the outside of the hub. This enabled the rear axle to be fully supported as the number of gears on the rear cassette increased.

Screw-on gears have the rear-axle bearings inboard of the rear block. They have two big disadvantages: firstly the bearings are inboard of the sprockets, so the axle isn't fully supported; and secondly all the rider's torque is transmitted to the tyres through the threads on the hub. This can make screw-on freewheels incredibly difficult to remove. And unlike the cassette system, a whole host of special tools are required. Each manufacturer has a unique tool that engages with the freewheel. There are at least four different tools required for freewheels that require a peg-type tool and three types of splined tool.

Single-speed bikes use a simple screw-on sprocket, complete with the freewheel ratchet mechanism. These are removed in the same manner as a screw-on rear block. On track bikes and 'fixies' (a road version of a track bike), the sprocket may be screwed on and then held in place with a lockring that has a left-hand thread to stop the sprocket unwinding. Some systems have a slide-on sprocket that is held in place with a lockring. Conversion kits are also available to run a single sprocket on a freehub body.

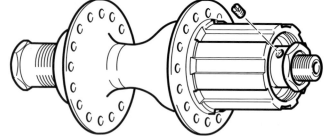

CAMPAGNOLO REAR HUB
Campagnolo freehub bodies require the removal of a small grub screw and a locknut before they can be removed.

SHIMANO REAR HUB
This drawing shows how a freehub body moves the bearings outboard. On a freewheel system, the axle bearings are either side of the spoke-mounting flange.

Removing a cassette

1 This is the locking ring on a Shimano cassette. Most hub manufacturers have adopted the Shimano system. Only Campagnolo use their own unique locking ring.

2 A chain whip will be required to hold the cassette and a special tool will be needed to loosen the locking ring. Loosening the locking ring calls for a reasonable amount of effort.

3 Turn the lockring tool anticlockwise to release it. You may hear a clicking sound as the ring releases – this is the serrated underside of the lockring sliding free from the freehub.

4 Remove the lockring. Some may have a very thin washer beneath. Recover the washer where fitted.

5 Remove the cassette as a single unit, or remove each sprocket in turn, noting any spacers fitted between them. The larger sprockets are often riveted together as one complete unit.

6 The freehub body with the sprockets removed.

FREEHUB BODY
The rear axle and bearings must be removed before the freehub can be removed. There are no serviceable parts on Shimano freehubs – if there's a problem it must be replaced as a complete unit.

CASSETTE QUALITY
Both these cassettes are new. However, the one on the left with the larger rings mounted on a separate spider arm is a far better quality item. It's also a lot lighter than the one on the right.

CAMPAGNOLO LOCKRINGS
Campagnolo use their own unique design and you'll need a specific Campagnolo lockring tool to remove their cassette.

Removing a screw-on freewheel

1 Remove the axle nut or quick release. Check that you have the correct tool and that it's a secure fit.

2 Fit the removal tool and refit the axle nut or quick release, finger-tight only. The best option is to mount the tool in a vice and rotate the wheel.

3 If no vice is available, use an adjustable spanner, or better still a large socket. Once the freewheel starts to move, slacken the axle nut or quick release as you unscrew the freewheel.

4 When you come to refit the freewheel, or when fitting a new one, use plenty of copper-based anti-seize compound on the threads.

Some older screw-on freewheels have removable sprockets. These enabled owners to alter ratios and replace worn sprockets. Replacement sprockets are no longer available.

SPECIAL TOOLS FOR SCREW-ON FREEWHEELS

Only ever attempt to remove the freewheel with the correct tool. If you think there's any chance of the tool (or you) slipping, cover the block with clean rags to prevent injury. If the complete hub rotates and the spokes distort, try applying penetrating fluid and leaving the wheel overnight. If that fails then consider replacing the entire wheel and block.

WHEN YOU NEED TO DO THIS:
- Cassettes and rear sprockets will require replacement if the chain is worn and has been neglected.
- When you fancy a change of gear ratio.
- If the freehub body requires attention.

TIME:
- Fifteen minutes to replace a cassette once the wheel is removed. Screw-on blocks can be notoriously difficult to release from the hub. Allow at least 30 minutes for screw-on sprockets.

DIFFICULTY: 🔧🔧🔧🔧
- Cassettes are simple to remove with the right tools, screw-on sprockets are problematic. Indeed, they're sometimes impossible to remove without destroying the wheel.

Single-speed sprockets

1 This is a 'flip-flop' hub – one side takes a fixed sprocket, the other side takes a freewheel sprocket. Simply flip the wheel around in the dropouts to change from fixed to freewheel.

2 To fit the freewheel, screw it on to the hub. Note that two thread sizes are common on single-speed hubs: BMX bikes tend to use a metric thread (M30X1); all others are English thread (1.37in X 24 TPI).

3 Fixed wheels are screwed on clockwise and then a clockwise locking collar is fitted.

4 To remove a fixed wheel, first remove the locking ring with the correct tool and then use a chain whip to remove the sprocket.

5 This Miche system requires an adaptor and a standard locking ring. It allows quick sprocket changes once the adaptor is fitted.

CHAIN TENSIONER DEVICE

This chain tensioner fits into the gear hanger and allows a single-speed set-up to work with bikes that have vertical dropouts. If you're converting a bike with a freehub cassette, a single-speed conversion kit will also be needed.

Chainsets and cranks

Most bikes fitted with an alloy crankset and cotterless cranks will have replaceable chainrings fitted. Each ring is held in place by either four or five special chainring bolts that require a special spanner or two hex keys to tighten or loosen them. On a double-ring set-up, the bolts will normally clamp both rings to the crank arm. On a typical triple-ring chainset, the low gear – the 'granny ring' – mounts directly to the crank arm with its own set of bolts. Mountain bikes tend to use a four-bolt crankset and road bikes a five-bolt crankset, but this isn't always the case.

Most chainrings will have a ramped profile and maybe riveted-on pins on the inner edge of the ring, to help the derailleur lift the chain on to the next ring. These aren't required on the smallest chainring though. Cheap chainrings may be pressed steel, have no shifting ramps and be riveted to the crank arm. These aren't replaceable and when worn a new crankset will be required.

When replacing chainrings, the large ring always has a small peg fitted. This must sit directly behind the crank arm. It's there to stop the chain dropping into the gap between the crank arm and the chainring. The other rings will have a mark on them to show their correct positioning. For smooth shifting it's important that these are fitted correctly. The other important thing to know when replacing chainrings is the bolt circle diameter (BCD), as this dictates the size of ring and the number of teeth on the chainring. A typical Shimano four-bolt triple crankset has a BCD of 104mm for the two large rings and 64mm for the 'granny ring'. This set-up can accommodate a 44/32- or 48/36-tooth outer ring combination and a 26- or 22-tooth 'granny ring'.

A road double-ring crankset may have a BCD of 130mm, capable of running a 39- or 42-tooth inner ring and up to a 56-tooth outer ring. The table shows how to calculate the BCD from the chainrings.

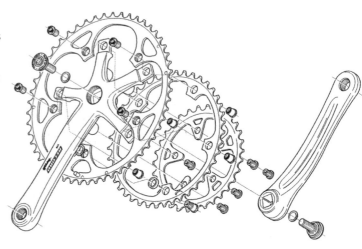

This is a five-arm triple chainset for a square-taper bottom bracket, an ideal chainset for a touring bike. Note the small peg on the big chainring. This must be fitted behind the crank arm.

TYPICAL ROAD CHAINSET
This is a typical five-arm road chainset. It has a BCD of 110mm and is fitted with a 48-tooth outer ring and a 34-tooth inner ring. This set-up is often referred to as a compact chainset because it uses a 48/34 double ring rather than the traditional 52/39 combination of chainrings.

Removing chainrings

1 The large chainring can often be removed with the chainset on the bike. Loosen each bolt a half-turn in order. Continue until they're all loose.

2 Remove the special chainring bolt. These mostly have a hex head, but torx-headed bolts are now fitted to some chainsets.

3 Check for any washers or spacers and lift the chainring over the crank arm.

4 On triple chainsets, the small ('granny') ring is usually mounted separately.

BOLT CIRCLE DIAMETER

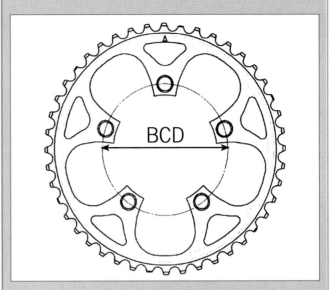

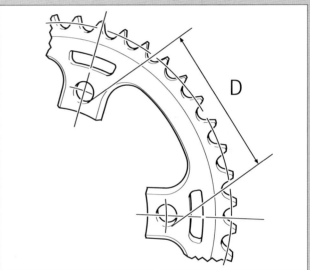

If you're sourcing replacement chainrings or are considering a change of gear ratios you'll need to know the bolt circle diameter (BCD). Remove the ring and measure the distance (D), then use the table to check the BCD.

FIVE-BOLT CHAINSET		FOUR-BOLT CHAINSET	
D (mm)	BCD (mm)	D (mm)	BCD (mm)
34.1	58	41.0	58
43.5	74	45.3	64
50.6	86	48.1	68
55.3	94	72.1	102
67.7	110	73.5	104
71.7	122	79.2	112
76.5	130	103.2	146
79.4	135		
84.7	144		

Removing chainsets and cranks

Recent changes have seen the introduction of a series of competing methods of locking the cranks to the bottom bracket. For many years cranks were either attached with cotter pins or used the square taper design pioneered by Stronglight of France. Cotter pins are rarely seen on modern bikes. Instead, you may find square taper cranks referred to as 'cotter-less', simply because they were introduced after 'cottered' cranks.

The introduction of a patented splined crank by Shimano to replace the square taper led to the introduction of various competing standards, including Truvativ's 'Powerspline' with its 12 splines. An open standard has also been developed by Truvativ, Race Face and the King cycle group. This design, known as ISIS, has ten splines compared to the eight of Shimano's 'Octalink'.

The latest development in cranks is to move the bearings outside the bottom-bracket shell and have the spindle as a part of the chainset rather than part of the bottom bracket. This is the system used by Shimano's popular 'Hollowtech II' chainset and Campagnolo's 'Ultra-Torque', amongst others.

If you're just replacing the chainset and not the bottom bracket and it's not square taper, always stick with the same manufacturer for replacements. This will avoid any compatibility issues.

Most chainsets will require a special tool to pull the crank off the splines or square taper. Though similar, two different tools will be required for square taper chainsets and splined chainsets. Both use a fine thread in the crank arm to locate the tool. The fine nature of the thread can often lead to problems as it's all too easy to strip out the threads from the soft alloy crank arm. Always lubricate and clean the threads in the crank arm before installing the special puller. A considerable amount of force may be required to pull the cranks off. This is especially true for square taper cranks that have been on a

bike for any length of time. If you think you're in danger of stripping the threads in the crank arm, then stop and remove the puller. Turn the bike on its side and apply plenty of penetrating fluid to the crank. Leave the fluid to penetrate, overnight if required. If the cranks still refuse to move, you can gently warm the crank arm with a hair dryer or hot-air gun. The differential expansion between the alloy crank and the steel axle often breaks the bond between them.

If you do strip the threads in the crank arm, it's possible to remove the chainset with an automotive-type two- or three-legged puller. You'll need to remove the chainrings to fit the puller on the drive side. This may destroy the chainset, but it will remove the crank arms.

When fitting square taper cranks, some controversy surrounds the lubrication of the taper. Should it be assembled dry or lubricated? Lubricating it guarantees the fixing bolt will pull the crank arm fully on to the taper; assembling it dry guarantees very close contact between crank arm and taper – Campagnolo always said that the built up grease on a mechanic's hands provided sufficient lubrication. Whichever method you choose, always recheck the security of the fixing bolt after a short ride and then after, say, 100 miles.

This is a square taper chainset from Stronglight, the company that invented the square taper crank.

Removing square taper chainsets

SPECIAL TOOLS
Two types of puller are in common use. The narrow-headed one fits square taper cranks; the wider-headed tool fits splined bottom brackets.

1 If fitted, remove the dust seal with a screwdriver or peg spanner. Many have the dust seal as part of the fixing bolt.

2 Clean and inspect the crank arm threads and lubricate the special puller before fitting it.

3 Take your time to fit the puller correctly. The fine thread makes cross-threading a possibility.

4 Hold the crank arm and tighten up the puller with a spanner that fits properly. Some pullers have the provision for a large hex key to be used instead of a spanner.

5 Screw in the puller until the crank comes off. Repeat the process for the opposite side.

Race Face self-extracting crank

1 Clutch the crank arm with your right hand and place an 8mm Allen key into the compression cap with your left hand.

2 Remove the compression cap and put to one side.

3 Use a square-tapered bottom-bracket tool and carefully thread onto the inside of the crank.

4 Don't over-tighten the tool as it's a pain to remove from the crank afterwards. Just enough to gain a grip.

5 The crank will now slowly come off onto the tool.

6 Remove the tool and remove the chain.

7 When putting the crank back on, remember to keep crank arms in the correct 'opposite' position.

TOOLS NEEDED
You'll need an 8mm Allen key, grease for when you replace the crank and a square-taper bottom-bracket tool.

Sram self-extracting crank

1 When loosening the crank, the bolt will go from tight to loose to tight. When you reach that final 'tight' position, keep going. The crank will come off.

2 Note position of washers and spacers for reapplying crank. Also grease the insides.

3 Be gentle when screwing back on – you don't want to mess up the threads. And make sure crank arms are in the correct position.

TOOLS NEEDED
An 8mm or 10mm Allen key depending on your crank. You also need a good dollop of grease.

Early Shimano 'XTR' chainset

1 Early Shimano 'XTR' and 'Dura-Ace' chainsets used an external bearing system and an 'Octalink'-splined spindle. A special tool (TL-FC35) is needed for these.

2 Remove the dust cover with the peg side of the tool. Note this is a left-hand thread. Turn clockwise to loosen. Clean and lubricate the threads of the crank and install the tool.

3 Turn the tool anticlockwise to tighten. The tool acts as a bearing surface for the main crank bolt to push against as it's removed. In effect it turns the 'XTR' into a self-extracting crank.

4 An 8mm hex key is now passed through the tool. Turn the hex key anticlockwise to remove the crank arm. This will be tight to start with.

5 Remove the special tool from the crank arm. Loosen the 2.5 hex key and wind the adjustable collar all the way back to the rear face of the crank arm.

6 Refit the crank arm. Tighten the 8mm hex bolt to the specified torque of 50Nm and refit the dust seal. Use the pegs on the special tool to fully tighten the dust seal.

7 If available, use special tool TL-FC17 to remove the play from the bearings. It should be possible to do this without the special tool, as the collar just rests against the bearing. Rock the crank arms and rotate the collar until all the play has disappeared. Tighten the hex screw on the collar.

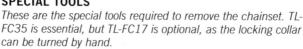

SPECIAL TOOLS
These are the special tools required to remove the chainset. TL-FC35 is essential, but TL-FC17 is optional, as the locking collar can be turned by hand.

Shimano 'Hollowtech II' chainset

Shimano's 'Hollowtech II' chainset, with external bottom bracket bearings, is an attempt to increase stiffness and resist twisting at the bottom bracket, whilst still being usable on all bikes until very recently. By moving the bearings to the outside of the bottom bracket shell the diameter of the spindle can be increased without reducing the size of the bearings.

If you upgrade your bike to an external bearing system, the face of the bottom-bracket shell should be machined flat with a suitable facing tool. This is an expensive tool, so facing the bottom bracket is best left to your local bike shop.

1 Before starting work, move the front derailleur over to the smallest chainring. Slacken the two crank-arm pinch bolts and, using either the correct tool or a very large screwdriver, remove the plastic end-cap.

2 Fully slacken off the two pinch bolts, loosening each one half a revolution alternately.

3 For clarity, we removed the pinch bolts and the plastic spacer completely, but you'll only need to slacken off the bolts enough to remove the crank arm.

4 Remove the crank arm to expose the outboard bearing. There will normally be an O-ring fitted to the inboard side of the crank arm. Check to make sure that this isn't left behind on the spindle.

5 Use a soft-faced mallet to drive out the chainset. Unhook the chain from the small chainring as the chainset is removed.

6 With the chainset removed, inspect the chainrings for damage, paying close attention to the condition of the splines on the spindle. Refit the chainset and crank arm. Use the special tool to pull the non-drive crank arm into position.

7 Tighten the pinch bolts evenly in turn. Use a torque wrench for the final tightening. Note that we've removed the end-cap to show that the crank arm is correctly located on the spindle.

Campagnolo 'Ultra-Torque' chainset

1 A 10mm hex key and a long-reach 10mm ring spanner are required to remove the centre locking bolt. Firmly locate the hex key and spanner.

2 Loosen and then remove the locking bolt. Expect to use a reasonable amount of force here, as the bolt is tightened to 42Nm.

3 Pull out the left-hand crank. The crank is removed complete with the bearing.

4 Remove the wavy washer from the bearing cup. It may have come out with the crank, so check there if it appears to be missing.

5 Remove the safety spring clip from the drive-side crank and remove the crank. Recover the wavy washer.

CAMPAGNOLO SAFETY CLIP
This safety clip must be fitted to the drive-side crank. Don't ride the bike without this clip in position.

CAMPAGNOLO HIRTH COUPLING
Campagnolo's 'Ultra-Torque' chainsets feature a two-part spindle joined at the centre with a Hirth coupling. This provides a strong, self-centring joint, but is expensive to manufacture so is only found on the top-of-the-range chainsets. Because the coupling is symmetrical it's possible to align the chainset off-centre.

One-piece chainsets

Often found on kids' bikes and entry-level BMX bikes, these use an oversize bottom bracket shell. Often referred to as Ashtabula chainsets, they're strong and cost-effective. Their weak point is often the poor sealing of the bottom-bracket bearings.

Adjusting the play in these bearings can be time-consuming, as it can be difficult to hold the inner race steady whilst the locking ring is tightened. A little trial and error will be required to get the cranks running smoothly with no play in them.

Newer BMX bikes tend to use a two- or three-piece chainset. These tend to be unique to each manufacturer with very little standardisation. Some require a bottom-bracket shell that's threaded, others use a press-fit bearing system.

1 The left-hand pedal must be removed to service one-piece chainsets. A large adjustable spanner can be used to release the bearing lockring. Turn clockwise to remove.

2 Next, release the bearing cup. Some have slots provided and can be removed by tapping gently with a blunt cold chisel, other types require the use of a peg or pin spanner.

3 Fully remove the bearing cup and feed the one-piece crank through the bottom-bracket shell. If the caged bearings are left behind in the shell, remove them before you remove the crank assembly.

4 If the bearing cups are worn, they can be driven out of the frame with a suitable punch. Fit them by pressing them home with a headset press or in a vice, or use a length of threaded bar and some suitable sockets.

BMX chainsets

1 Slacken off the rear wheel nuts and then loosen the main crank-arm pinch bolt. This can be very tight on systems that rely on a single bolt.

2 Slacken off and remove the end bolt from the crank spindle.

3 The crank arm should now slide off the spindle. On some types, you may have to remove the pinch bolt completely before you can pull off the arm itself.

4 As the crank arm is removed, recover the washers and spacers, noting the order in which they're fitted.

5 Rotate the crank, unhook the chain and push out the spindle complete with the chainring and drive-side crank.

6 This chainset uses press-fit bearings in the bottom-bracket shell. There's a floating spacer between the two bearings in the bottom bracket that needs to be moved to one side to enable the bearings to be removed with a suitable drift or punch.

7 The chainring can be removed if damaged. Protect the arm if necessary and place the chainset in a vice or workbench. Loosen the hex bolt to remove the chainring.

8 When refitting the chainset, the spindle end bolt is used to preload the bearings in the bottom bracket shell. Adjust the preload so that the crank arms spin freely with no play. When this is correct tighten the crank-arm pinch bolt fully. Refit the chain and adjust the chain tensioner.

WHEN YOU NEED TO DO THIS:
- When you need to access the bottom bracket.
- If the chainrings are worn.
- If the crank arms are worn or the pedal mounting threads are damaged.

TIME:
- Allow at least an hour for all but the most straightforward of chainsets.

DIFFICULTY:
- Removing square taper chainsets can be hard work, but most of the other types are removed fairly easily.

Gear changers

More commonly referred to as 'shifters', gear changers come in many styles. Where once downtube shifters dominated, they've now been usurped by the more proficient gear-and-brake lever system. Flat-bar bikes may have simple non-indexed thumb-shifters, twist-grip shifters or dual-trigger shifters. Each of the major component manufacturers have their own systems. Shimano have 'STi' for drop-handlebar bikes, 'Rapid Fire' and thumb-shifters for flat-bar bikes and Di2 buttons for electronic groupsets.

Sram have 'Gripshift' rotary shifters and trigger-based shifters for flat-bar bikes. For drop-handlebar bikes, they have their own combined brake and gear system called 'DoubleTap' and eTap for electric groupsets. Campagnolo supply shifters for drop-handlebar bikes called 'Ergopower' and EPS for their electronic alternative.

You'll also find triathlon bikes or time-trial bikes will feature bar-end shifters. These are levers on the end of aerobars that mean the cyclist can remained slipstreamed while shifting gears.

WHEN YOU NEED TO DO THIS:
■ Every six months or so for a bike in regular use.

TIME:
■ Ten minutes for a complete lube. If you decide to remove the levers for thorough cleaning add another 15 minutes for flat-bar shifters and at least an hour for drop-handlebars gear levers.

DIFFICULTY: 🔧🔧
■ Lubrication is straightforward.

Flat-bar shifters

1 This indexed thumb-shifter is best lubricated with oil from an aerosol can. Rotate the shifter while applying the lubricant.

2 Remove the cable access screw for a quick lube. There are many plastic parts inside most shifters, so always use a lubricant that's plastic friendly. Most are, but do check first.

3 On this Rapidfire Plus shifter remove the gear cable and lower cover for a proper clean-out. A plastic-friendly synthetic grease should be used to lubricate the moving parts.

4 This style of rotary shifter can be lubricated through the cable cover. A small amount of lubricant will go a long way.

5 Most classic road-bike shifters are mounted on the down tube. Older touring bikes may have them mounted on the quill stem. Slacken off the friction adjuster and apply a small amount of lubricant.

Combined brake and gear levers

1 Slacken off the gear cable at the brake and apply a few drops of wax-based lubricant to the pivot points. If possible allow a few drops to dribble down the brake cable and gear cables.

2 The same technique can be used on Sram 'DoubleTap' levers. Operate the brake a few times to allow the lubricant to penetrate to the pivot points.

3 Loosen the gear cable at the front or rear mech and roll back the brake lever hoods. Apply a little lubricant to the gear cable and the gear-change mechanism.

4 Roll back the lever hoods and use a similar method to lubricate Campagnolo's 'Ergopower' levers.

Bottom brackets

Cup and axle bottom brackets

For many years, adjustable bottom brackets were the most common type. They were fitted to all sorts of bikes, including top-of-the-range racing models. They're cheap to produce but time-consuming to assemble – especially on the production line. Their biggest weak point is the lack of a decent sealing system. The grease in the bearings soon becomes an emulsified mess, and rapid wear of the bearings, cups and axles ensues. The good news is that most bikes now come with a 'sealed' or 'cartridge' (as they're sometimes called) bottom bracket as standard. And if you do still have an adjustable bottom bracket, it's relatively inexpensive to upgrade.

All that said, if you have an adjustable bottom bracket and it's in good condition, it can be greased and refitted. Next it will require adjustment. Screw in the adjustable cup until a slight drag can be felt. There should be no play in the spindle at this point. If you can only remove the play by further tightening of the adjustable cup, consider replacing the complete assembly. If all is well fit the locking collar and, holding the adjustable cup steady, tighten it. Check that the spindle still turns smoothly and refit the cranks. It may take a few tries to get this perfect.

These are the tools required to service a typical adjustable bottom bracket.

Alternative tools

A pair of sliding joint pliers can be used on the locking collar. Take care not to damage the paint on the frame, though.

Two short screws can be used instead of a pin spanner. Turn them with a screwdriver.

A large adjustable spanner can be used to undo the fixed cup.

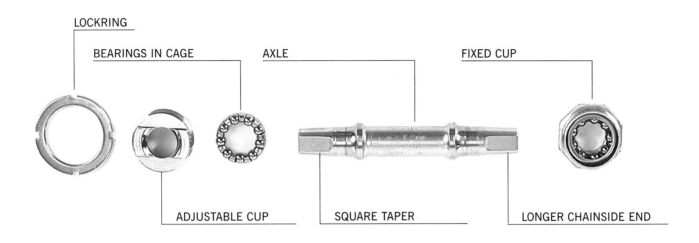

LOCKRING

BEARINGS IN CAGE

AXLE

FIXED CUP

ADJUSTABLE CUP

SQUARE TAPER

LONGER CHAINSIDE END

Removing an adjustable bottom bracket

1 Remove the cranks from both sides. Working on the non-drive side, slacken and remove the locking collar. Use a 'C' spanner or punch. The collar is removed *anticlockwise*.

2 A pin spanner is used to remove the adjustable cup. The cup is removed *clockwise*.

3 You may find loose bearings or a set of caged bearings inside the cup. Take care to catch any bearings that fall out. If loose bearings are fitted you'll have 11 bearings per side.

4 Pull out the axle (spindle) and clean it with a rag and degreaser. Some systems may have a plastic sleeve fitted over the axle.

5 Next remove the fixed cup. This has a left-hand thread and must be removed *clockwise* (remembering 'Drivel' will help – 'drive equals left'). Clean and inspect the fixed cup.

6 If the cups and axle are in good condition, apply a little waterproof grease and fit 11 new ball bearings. If the bearings were the caged type (with nine bearings) then it's possible to fit 11 new loose bearings instead.

WORN COMPONENTS

After cleaning the component parts, carefully inspect them. On these cups the surface coating has worn through. The axle is pitted and worn on the bearing surface. These parts all require replacement. Consider upgrading to a sealed bottom bracket in this instance.

Sealed bottom brackets

Until the advent of the external bearing bottom bracket and the rise and rise of BB30 and PF30 bottom brackets, sealed bottom brackets dominated the mid- to high-end bike market. The universal square taper was the market leader for many years and is still found on many mid-range and lower-end bikes.

In the search for a stiffer interface, Shimano and others came up with a splined crank mounting system. Shimano call theirs 'Octalink', Truvativ have 'Powerspline' and FSA have 'Powerdrive'. Add to this the open ISIS (International Standard Interface System) spline and the choice of bottom bracket becomes a minefield. The best advice will always be to stick with the same brand if you're replacing just the bottom bracket. The appendix lists some commonly available sizes.

BOTTOM BRACKETS IN BRIEF

Conventional threaded
Threaded bottom brackets are compatible with the largest range of cranks, and are a good addition to any bike because they isolate the bearing from the frameset and so make it easier to maintain if you have an issue. Crank designs that fit include Shimano Hollowtech II.

Cartridge bottom brackets
Otherwise known as sealed bottom brackets, these feature a small diameter axle and internal bearings sealed in a metal cylinder, which screws into the bottom-bracket shell as a single unit. Pedal axles for cartridge bottom brackets may be square-taper or splined at the interface with the cranks, while some chainsets use integrated axles that aren't designed for use with cartridge bottom brackets.

Press-fit bottom brackets
Bearings are pressed directly into the frame, either in aluminium cups or into races that are moulded into the structure of the frame.

Removing an 'Octalink' bottom bracket

1 Though the pictures show an 'Octalink' bottom bracket, other types are removed in a similar manner.

2 Fit the adaptor to the non-drive side. The splines that the tool locates on aren't very deep, so firmly locate the tool and support it with your other hand.

3 With the tool in position and supported, turn it *anticlockwise* to remove the locking collar from the bottom bracket.

4 With the collar removed, move over to the drive side and locate the tool.

5 Turn the tool *clockwise* to undo the bottom bracket (remembering 'Drivel' will help – 'drive equals left').

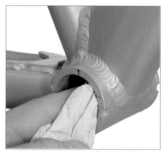

6 Unscrew and then remove the complete sealed bottom bracket.

7 With the bottom bracket removed, clean and inspect the condition of the threads. If they're damaged, specialist help will be needed. It's possible for a specialist repairer to drill out the shell and fit a threaded sleeve into the frame.

8 Cover the threads with grease or an anti-seize compound and screw the replacement bottom bracket in. Stop when you're about three or four threads from fully home.

External bearing bottom brackets

The major drawback with traditional adjustable and sealed bottom brackets has always been the maximum diameter of the spindle that can be fitted into the bracket shell. External bearing brackets move the bearings to the outside of the shell, allowing a large, hollow spindle to be fitted. This reduces weight and increases stiffness. A stiff, light bottom bracket allows the rider to transmit more power directly to the drivetrain.

Most manufacturers have further increased stiffness and lost more weight by bonding the spindle to the drive-side crank arm. Some systems still have a separate spindle, though.

External bottom brackets will fit all standard bottom-bracket shells. Spacing washers are provided to adapt them to the various shell widths. If you're upgrading from an internal to an external system the surface of the bracket shell may require facing. This is a job for your local bike shop, as the tool required is far too expensive for the home mechanic to purchase. The tool screws into the bottom bracket and a cutter removes a small amount of material from the edge of the shell. This trues up the faces and ensures that they're parallel to each other and at 90° to the screw threads.

1 Remove the non-drive crank arm and then the drive-side crank and chainrings.

2 Locate the correct tool on the bearing and remove the bearing.

3 The direction for tightening is clearly marked on these Shimano outboard bearings. Reverse this to remove the bearing.

4 Unscrew the bearing and remove it, complete with the plastic sleeve.

5 We constructed a simple mounting block for the bottom bracket removal tool and mounted it on a workbench to enable us to remove the bearings from the bracket.

6 With the jig firmly mounted on the workbench we used a punch to drive out the old bearings.

7 With a suitable diameter hole drilled in our jig, we mounted the bottom bracket in it and used a clamp and socket to press the new bearing into the bracket.

8 This type of external bottom bracket has an O-ring and top hat washer that must be replaced once the bearing has been pressed into the bearing cup. Note that Shimano external (Hollowtech) BBs cannot be deconstructed and new bearings fitted.

BB30 bottom brackets

The external bearing bottom bracket was one solution to increasing stiffness and reducing weight, but its main drawback was an increase in the theoretical 'Q' factor. Simply put, the 'Q' factor is the distance the pedals are from the centreline of the bottom bracket. This affects cornering ability and the pedal stroke.

Cannondale decided to address this problem and came up with the open standard BB30, where 30 represents the diameter of the chainset spindle. It's free for any manufacturer to use and has proved incredibly popular, as the bearings are a press-fit into the frame,

which cuts right down on assembly time. Another advantage is the increased surface area of the shell, which allows frame builders more space to fit oversized frame tubes.

Shimano have yet to take up the standard, but adaptors can fit Shimano's 'Hollowtech II' chainsets. A sleeve is also available that's bonded into place and converts the BB30 back to a standard threaded bottom bracket.

BB30 bottom brackets are impressive, though the metal-on-metal interfaces can be prone to creaking.

1 Remove the chainset. This crank arm is the self-extracting type and no special tools are required.

2 Locate the gap between the ears of the internal circlip. Use a punch to drive out the bearing.

3 If necessary, use a scriber to rotate the internal circlip so that you can punch the opposite side of the bearing to remove it. This will ensure that the bearing is removed squarely and evenly from the bracket shell.

4 With the bearings removed, use a pair of circlip pliers or a scriber to remove the circlip. Fit new circlips and use old sockets and a length of threaded bar to draw the new bearings into the bottom bracket shell. Refit the chainset and crank arm. A bearing setting drift is also widely available to set BB30 bearings to exactly the right depth in the BB shell. Used in conjunction with a headset press or threaded bar it ensures that you don't press the bearings in too far and either damage the circlips, BB shell or both. Well worth investing in if you own a BB30 bike.

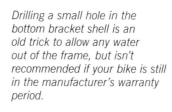

Drilling a small hole in the bottom bracket shell is an old trick to allow any water out of the frame, but isn't recommended if your bike is still in the manufacturer's warranty period.

WHEN YOU NEED TO DO THIS:
■ Only required when
play develops in the bottom bracket or it seizes up.

TIME:
■ Allow at least an hour for most bottom brackets.

DIFFICULTY: 🔧🔧🔧
■ With a set of quality specialist tools removing bottom brackets should present no major difficulties. The biggest problem is often dealing with rusted threads in the shell.

Replacing a PF30 bottom bracket

PF30 (or Press-Fit 30) bottom brackets are similar to BB30 in that the position of the bearings and bearing locations are identical. However, the PF30 features composite cups, which allows for greater frame tolerances. This means that bicycle manufacturers require much less precise machining of the bottom-bracket shell area.

Proponents argue that they're just as good as BB30 bottom brackets, especially as they feature an integrated sealing system that should prolong its life. And when it reaches the end of its time, it's also cost-effective to replace. Critics counter by saying those frame tolerances – twice as much as those using BB30 – are too large and question the quality of the PF30 bottom bracket and respective frame.

1 With crank removed, clean around the entrance of the bottom bracket so you have easy access.

2 Tools specific to the job include a headset press and PF30 tool (this one is from Park Tool). You also need a rubber-ended mallet.

3 If this doesn't remove one end, try from the other side as the PF30 bottom bracket is in two parts.

4 If that's successful, return to the drive side, fit the end into the shoulder and slide the 'slider' of the PF30 tool up to the remaining bottom bracket. This gives greater purchase for striking with the mallet.

5 The new bottom bracket is again in two parts. They are left (L) and right (R) specific so make sure they're the right way around.

6 Attach the headset press to the bottom bracket. Make sure you have the correct spacers fitted to your tool because you need to apply pressure evenly and not at an odd angle.

TOOLS NEEDED
Specialised tools are required including a headset press and PF30 tool. You also need a rubber-ended mallet.

7 Gradually wind the tool so the bottom bracket is inserted. But keep checking and don't over-tighten.

8 As soon as you feel the tool arms come to a stop, this is generally the correct position.

9 Put the washers and spacers back on. Now your bottom bracket is ready to accommodate the crank.

Hub gears

Always popular on the Continent, in recent years hub gears have made a bit of a comeback in the UK on commuter and folding bikes like those from Brompton. Gears now range from three to 14 and the hubs are produced by Shimano, Sturmey-Archer, Sram and Rohloff. Shimano have a large range with three, four, seven and eight speeds available in the 'Nexus' range and eight and 11 speeds in the 'Alfine' range. Sturmey-Archer have two-, three-, four-, five- and eight-speed models. Sram offer three- and nine-speed models and Rohloff have a 14-speed hub. Many of the hubs are also available with integral brakes or disc brakes. In addition some have a dynamo option.

The beauty of hub gears is their reliability. Little maintenance is required to keep them running smoothly for many years. All that's normally required is adjustment of the gear selection and replacement of the gear cables.

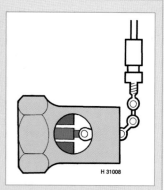

STURMEY-ARCHER ADJUSTMENT
This is the standard Sturmey-Archer hub nut with an inspection hole for aligning the selector rod with the end of the axle. With second gear selected adjust the selector rod until it's in the position shown.

The five-speed Sturmey-Archer hub is adjusted in a similar manner to the three-speed hub, except that you align the blue or red notch in the selector rod with the end of the axle.

Removing the back wheel

1 All hub-geared bikes require the gear selector cable to be disconnected before the back wheel can be removed. On this classic Sturmey-Archer hub, release the knurled locking nut and unscrew the cable adjuster. You may also need to remove any chain guard fitted.

2 Slacken both wheel nuts with a spanner, then undo them the rest of the way with your fingers. To prevent the axle turning, special washers fit around the axle and into the frame. Place the wheel nuts and washers to one side.

3 Push the axle forward with your thumbs, if possible. Alternatively push the tyre forward whilst supporting the bike frame with one hand. Lift the chain off the sprocket and place the wheel to one side.

4 When refitting, replace the shaped axle washers. Then do up the wheel nuts lightly, pulling the wheel back so that it's centralised, with about 12mm of play in the chain. Tighten the wheel nuts, giving each side a turn at a time, and refit the gear cable.

Sturmey-Archer cable adjustment

1 Newer bikes often have a shroud covering the cable adjuster. Remove the shroud and apply a few drops of oil to the chain links.

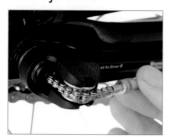

2 To remove the cable, place the gear shifter in top gear, unscrew the locking nut and then unthread the cable. Slacken off the cable clamp and fit a new cable. Clamp the outer in exactly the same place and reconnect the inner cable.

3 Some models will feature a guide pulley to reduce the friction and make gear selection easier. Select second gear and pedal a few revolutions. Look at the end of the axle.

4 Adjust the selector cable so that the control rod is flush with the end of the axle (see diagram). Tighten up the locking nut and take the bike for a short test ride. Make the adjustment again if necessary.

Sturmey-Archer eight-speed hub

BASIC ADJUSTMENT

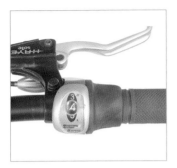

1 The new-style eight-speed hubs are normally fitted with a rotary gear changer. Select fourth gear to start the adjustment procedure.

2 This hub requires adjustment, as the yellow mark on the hub doesn't align with the yellow mark on the selector arm.

3 Release the knurled lock nut and adjust the cable tension until the alignment is correct.

4 This hub is now correctly adjusted, as the marks on the hub and selector align correctly. Tighten up the locking nut and test ride. Readjust if necessary.

REMOVING THE REAR WHEEL

1 Move the shifter to the eighth gear position and unhook the adjuster from the bracket on the chain stay. It has a keyhole fitting to allow easy removal.

2 The cable can now be unhooked from the selector. Slide the cable forward and unhook it.

3 Undo the hub nuts using a pair of 15mm ring spanners.

4 Next remove the lock washers from each side of the frame. Push the wheel forward to unhook the chain and then slide out the wheel.

5 To replace the wheel reverse the removal procedure. Refit the cable and slide the barrel adjuster back into place.

6 Pull the wheel back to tension the chain. Adjust the tension so that there's about 10mm of play in the chain. Adjust the gear selector cable and then test ride the bike.

On the Sturmey-Archer shifter remove the hex screw to lubricate the mechanism or replace the cable.

Shimano hub gears

Shimano produce a wide range of hub gears. They're currently available with three, four, seven, eight and 11 speeds. They may have coaster brakes, roller brakes or disc brakes fitted. They're all reliable and robust units that require little in the way of maintenance. Traditionally fitted to city and commuter bikes, they're gaining popularity with touring cyclists and off-road riders as the number of gear ratios increase. Most are operated by Shimano's 'RevoShift' rotary shifter, but their 'Rapid Fire' shifters are an option on some models.

CABLE ADJUSTMENT AND REPLACEMENT

1 Cable adjustment on Shimano 'Nexus' hub gears takes place with the shifter in the fourth gear position. The newer 'Alfine' hubs need the shifter set to the sixth gear.

2 Remove the three small crosshead screws from the bottom of the shifter.

3 On the top of the shifter, remove the cover. Cut the cable at a convenient point on an exposed section and then unhook the nipple and remove the cable.

4 At the rear wheel remove the small grub screw and pull the cable free. Feed in the new cable at the shifter end.

5 Screw in the barrel adjuster and feed the new cable around the three rollers in the shifter.

6 Feed the cable around the rear dropout and up through the cable clamp. Pull it firmly and tighten the clamp.

7 Check that the shifter is still in fourth gear and then use the barrel adjuster to align the two red marks on the hub. Take the bike for a short test ride and then recheck the alignment. Adjust again if necessary.

REMOVING THE BACK WHEEL

1 On Shimano hubs, engage first gear to slacken the cable.

2 At the rear remove the shroud that covers the hub nuts. Many bikes will also have a chain guard that will require removal. Free the outer cable and unhook the inner cable from the pulley.

3 Use a 15mm spanner to loosen and remove the hub nuts.

4 Remove the locking washers and push the wheel forward to unhook the chain.

WHEN YOU NEED TO DO THIS:
■ Adjustment of the gearchange will be required if the cable is worn or if the rear wheel has been removed and repositioned slightly differently.

TIME:
■ Fifteen minutes to adjust the indexing. Allow an hour to remove the rear wheel and adjust the gear selection.

DIFFICULTY:
■ Most hub gears have clearly identifiable marks to align the indexing correctly, so the task is fairly straightforward.

5 Remove the wheel. Refitting is a reversal of the removal procedure, but adjust (and renew if necessary) the gear selector cable.

ROHLOFF 'SPEEDHUB'
This precision German-manufactured 14-speed hub gear is the newest and latest incarnation of hub-gear technology. Unlike other hub gears the indexing is controlled internally. Once the control cables are installed no further adjustment is required. If the rear wheel requires removal then the cables are detached either with a simple bayonet fitting or via a thumbwheel.

Sram hub gears

Sram's purchase of the bicycle parts division of German company Sachs allowed them to add a hub gear to their product range. Originally know as the 'Torpedo', Sram now call these hubs 'T3' or 'i-Motion'. The 'Torpedo' brand name appears to be reserved for a hub that converts from fixed to free wheel (and back again) from a bar-mounted shifter.

Like Shimano, Sram offer their hubs with a selection of brake choices. Unlike Shimano they also offer the three-speed hub with a cassette and derailleur system. Sram call this 'DualDrive'.

WHEEL REMOVAL

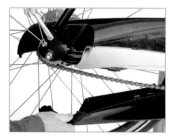

1 Many bikes that feature hub gears will have a chain guard of some description fitted. Where fitted remove the guard to access the rear-wheel nuts.

2 On some models you may have to remove most of the chain guard. This model doesn't require any tools to remove it.

3 Remove the hub nuts and lever out the axle locking nuts. These are a snug fit in the dropout and you may need to use an old screwdriver to release them.

4 Drop the wheel from the frame. On most 'i-Motion' hubs the gear selector cable is inboard of the chain stay. Twist and slide back the locking collar.

5 With the collar released, unhook the cable connector from the hub.

6 Unhook the chain from the sprocket and remove the wheel. Refitting is a reversal of the removal procedure, but check and adjust the gear cable if necessary.

This is Sram's 'T3' hub (formerly know as 'Torpedo') complete with a coaster brake.

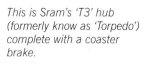

GEAR CABLE ADJUSTMENT: 'I-MOTION' HUBS

1 The 'i-Motion' nine-speed hub is adjusted with the gear selector in the sixth-gear position.

2 Use the gear shifter barrel adjuster to align the red and yellow marks on the rear hub.

3 Two sets of alignment marks are provided, above and below the chain stay.

GEAR CABLE ADJUSTMENT: THREE-SPEED HUBS

1 Select third gear or 'H'. Make sure the selector chain is fully screwed into the hub. Some models may have a guide pulley fitted to the hub.

2 The cable terminates with a quick release connector. Depress the clip to release the gear cable. The cable length can be adjusted with a small hex key if necessary.

3 Refit the connector and slide it up the selector chain, so that there's no play in the cable. The cable should be tight, but not pulling the selector chain. Slacken the hex key fitting and adjust the overall cable length if necessary.

Sram 'DualDrive'

This is a hybrid system that combines a three-speed hub with either an eight- or nine-speed cassette and a derailleur. All the gear-change functions are combined into one right-hand shifter. The rotary shifter controls the derailleur-driven gears and a sliding switch controls the internal hub gears. The gear selector cable has a quick release feature at the hub. Sram call this a 'Clickbox'.

To adjust the hub gears, select second gear – the middle position – and then rotate the barrel adjuster at the hub so that the yellow marks in the 'Clickbox' window align. The derailleur adjustment is exactly the same as a normal derailleur gear system – see pages 88–91 for a full explanation of derailleur gear adjustment procedures.

To remove the rear wheel, move the rotary shifter to the highest gear and the hub gear shifter to the low gear position (the single dot on the shifter diagram). Push the small button on the 'Clickbox' down and pull off the 'Clickbox'. Unscrew the hub gear selector rod and then remove the axle nuts and lock washers. Slide the wheel out and remove as a normal derailleur rear wheel. Refitting is a reversal of removal, but when the 'Clickbox' is in position push the button up from below.

The derailleur gear cable is replaced exactly the same as any derailleur-geared bike (see pages 84–85). To replace the hub gear cable remove the 'Clickbox' as described above for rear-wheel removal. Remove the end cover of the 'Clickbox' and release the cable clamp with a 4mm hex key. At the shifter screw the barrel adjuster fully home. Remove the cable cover and pull out the gear cable. Refitting is a reversal of this procedure, but after clamping the cable cut off the excess and carry out the adjustment procedure.

A standard Sram-style derailleur takes care of shifting of the derailleur gears. The derailleur is adjusted just like a normal derailleur gear system.

This is the single-shifter used on the 'DualDrive' system. The rotary 'Gripshift' controls the derailleur and the sliding switch controls the hub gears.

This is the 'DualDrive' hub assembly complete with quick release 'Clickbox'. The alignment marks can be seen through the small window. The small button releases the 'Clickbox' from the hub.

CHAPTER

CONTACT POINTS

In this chapter we look at the parts of the bike with which the rider is in contact. The contact points are important for your comfort and for cycling efficiency. Most can easily be adjusted or replaced to achieve a comfortable riding position. For many riders this may well be just a change of saddle and perhaps some new grips or bar tape.

Assuming the bike frame is the correct one, it's also possible to change the stem length and height, the fore-and-aft position of the saddle and even the length and layback of the seat post ('layback' is the distance between the seat rail clamp and the centreline of the seat post tube). For the serious cyclist it's also possible to change the crank length and pedal type.

If you have a bike with the confusingly named A-headset (often called an 'A'-head), which has a bearing and stem system fitted, a large range of stems are available.

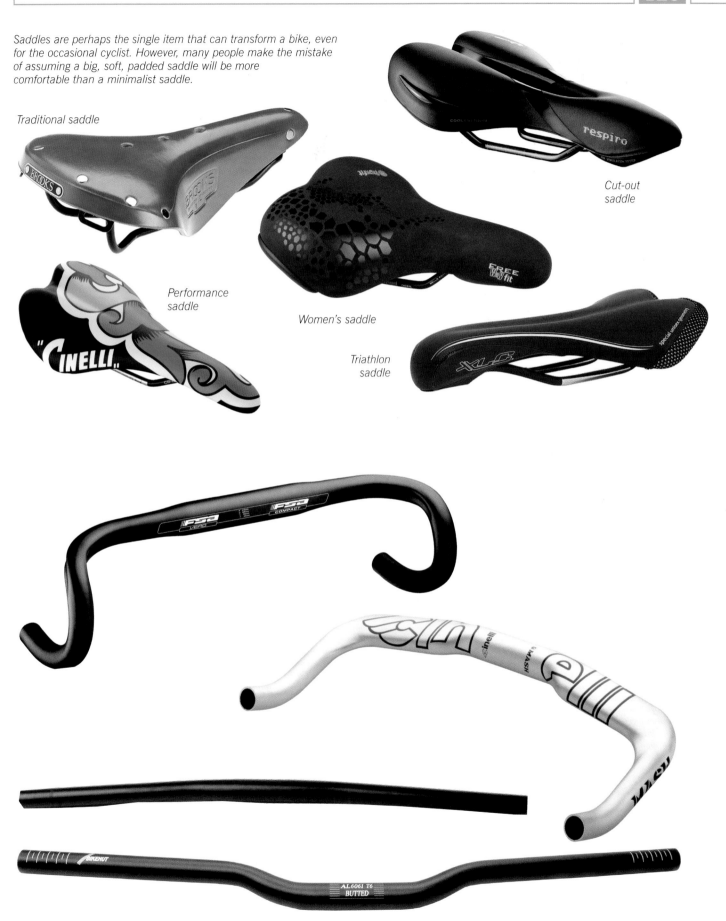

Saddles are perhaps the single item that can transform a bike, even for the occasional cyclist. However, many people make the mistake of assuming a big, soft, padded saddle will be more comfortable than a minimalist saddle.

Traditional saddle

Cut-out saddle

Performance saddle

Women's saddle

Triathlon saddle

Safety check

A quick check of the contact points is always worthwhile. The seat post and saddle mounting are highly stressed areas, especially with a compact frame and fully extended seat post. The same is also true of the stem and the handlebars. A check should be made at the seat post where it emerges from the frame, and at the handlebars close to the stem. These are areas where stress-related cracks may start.

Saddles that use a single bolt to mount to the seat post should have the bolt removed and checked occasionally. This is especially true where a steel bolt fits into an alloy clamp, as it's possible for galvanic corrosion to start here. The same corrosion may also be found on steel-framed bikes fitted with alloy seat posts.

If you're lucky enough to have carbon-fibre handlebars mounted on an aluminium stem, pay particular attention to the mounting bolts and the edges of the stem. If necessary use a file to remove any sharp edges from the stem, and always use a torque wrench to secure the handlebars.

1 Check closely for fractures where the seat post emerges from the frame. Check the saddle mounting bolts for security.

2 Seat-post clamps and pinch bolts should be checked. Pay particular attention to the top of the seat post tube where the clamp sits.

3 Check the security of the stem fixing bolts on 'A'-head stems.

4 On traditional quill stems, check the wedge fixing bolt.

5 When replacing the bar tape on drop handlebar bikes, it's worth checking the mounting band on the brake levers. The steel band can often bite deeply into aluminium alloy handlebars.

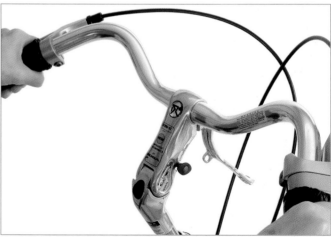

6 Check closely where the stem clamps the handlebars. Fractures can often start here. If you have an adjustable stem check the security of the mounting bolts.

The threaded fork steerer was always a problem in search of a solution – adjusting the steering bearings was a time-consuming and problematic job. The A-headset not only solved the adjustment problems but also allowed stems and handlebars to be easily swapped. It's also stiffer and far more secure than the traditional quill stem and lock-nut steering system.

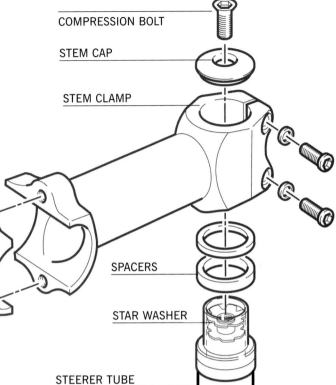

COMPRESSION BOLT

STEM CAP

STEM CLAMP

SPACERS

STAR WASHER

STEERER TUBE

This expanding wedge from British brand Hope is a neat way to remove and transfer A-head stems to a new bike.

SAFETY LINE

All traditional quill stems and seat posts will have an extension limit mark. Do not exceed this limit. If necessary change the stem or seat post for a longer one. One point to note is that on seat posts for bikes with interrupted or bent seat-post tubes, a previous owner may have cut down the post to make it low enough to ride. If this is the case, the limit mark will be meaningless. A good rule of thumb is to have *at least* 60mm of seat post below the clamp or pinch bolt, or that the end of the seatpost should clear the bottom weld/join of the toptube by at least 20mm.

Handlebars and stems

The stem connects the front forks to the handlebars. On traditional quill stems, an expanding wedge clamps the inside of the steerer tube. On the modern A-headset system, the stem clamps around the steerer tube. To adjust the height of a traditional quill stem, the wedge must first be loosened. On the A-headset system the height of the stem can be altered by adding or removing washers.

On old-style traditional quill stems, changing the handlebars was often a long and involved procedure, as only a single bolt clamped the handlebars in position. So to change the handlebars it was necessary to feed them through the stem clamp. Newer quill stems and 'A'-head stems have a removable front clamp. This makes changing handlebars relatively easy.

To replace the stem, first remove the handlebars by removing the front clamp. On old-style quill stems, the brake levers and bar tape will have to be removed and the handlebars threaded through the stem clamp. On 'A'-head stems, first remove the top cap bolt and then loosen the pinch bolts from the side of the stem. The stem can now be pulled off the steerer. On quill stems, loosen the wedge clamp bolt and tap it down. Rock the stem from side to side, then pull it up to release it from the steerer tube. You may need to apply penetrating fluid, as quill stems are notorious for corroding in position.

For many years handlebars were all one diameter, based on the traditional size of 1in (25.4mm). Newer handlebars and stems are described as 'oversize' or 'oversized'. These have a central diameter of $1^1/\!_8$in (31.8mm). Some old Italian handlebars have a central diameter of 26mm and BMX bikes have a central diameter of $^7/\!_8$in. The end diameter of traditional drop handlebars is $^{15}/\!_{16}$in (23.8mm). On flat-bar bikes the end diameter is $^7/\!_8$in (22.2mm).

Some city bikes may be fitted with a traditional road-style quill stem. These are adjusted in just the same way as standard quill stems.

ADJUSTABLE STEMS

These are fitted to some hybrid bikes. They allow you to adjust your riding position without replacing the stem.

First loosen the pinch bolt that clamps the stem to the steerer. Then loosen the upper bolt. The stem can now be moved up or down.

When you have the stem at the correct position, tighten the upper bolt and then tighten the clamp bolt. The type shown above is suitable for the A-headset system. Adjustable stems are also available for traditional quill-type steerers.

Removing the handlebar stem

2 On some quill-type stems, the wedge bolt is hidden below a plug. Remove the plug to access the bolt.

3 You'll need a long hex key to access the bolt. A socket set is very useful here. Alternatively use a ring spanner or piece of metal tube on the short leg of a standard hex key.

1 In the A-headset system, the stem is clamped to the outside of the steerer tube. A limited number of washers are often fitted below the stem, which allow a certain amount of height adjustment. However, the steerer must always be slightly below the top of the stem. If the steerer is flush with or above the stem, then it isn't possible to preload the headset bearings.

5 Quill stems that have been in place for a long time can be difficult to remove. Apply plenty of penetrating oil and rock the stem from side to side. Protect the stem with a block of wood and then try tapping it down as well.

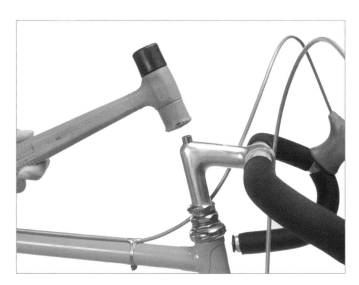

4 On older versions of the quill stem, you'll find an exposed hex bolt or socket-head hex. On both types slacken the bolt four or five turns and then tap it down to release the wedge and the bolt from the bottom of the stem.

Front-loading stems

1 Most modern stems now feature a removable front clamp. This may be held in place with either two or four bolts. Slacken each bolt a little at a time.

2 With the clamp removed, check for any damage to the handlebars. Clean the mounting surface with a wire brush, wet and dry and/or disc brake cleaner.

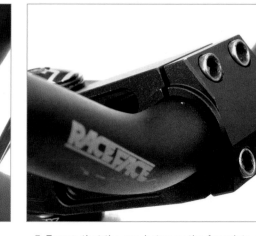

3 Apply anti-seize compound to the threads and refit the front plate. Tighten the mounting bolts evenly, checking that the gap between the stem and clamp is even. Note: many stems feature max torque figures. You can measure pressure via a torque wrench. Some face plate bolts, such as those found on Canyon bikes, require an uneven tensioning, but this is uncommon.

4 Ensure that the gap between the faceplate and the stem is even at the bottom and the top. On a four-bolt clamp always tighten the bolts evenly, in a diagonal sequence.

Extensions are available to raise the height of the stem. However, if you need to use a stem extension like this you may be on a bike that's really too small for you.

WHEN YOU NEED TO DO THIS:
■ When new components have been fitted.

TIME:
■ Five minutes to alter the position of the bars or stem.
■ Thirty minutes to an hour to replace handlebars, especially if you're replacing drop handlebars.

DIFFICULTY:
■ A-headset stems are straightforward, quill stems can often be rusted into position.

Removing handlebars

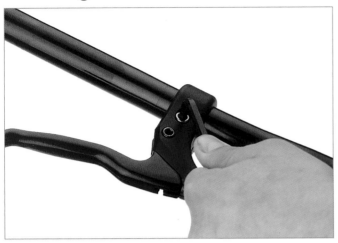

1 On flat-bar bikes with a single stem clamp bolt you must remove the brakes, grips and shifters. If you're only altering the angle of the bars then just slacken the brakes and shifters.

2 Slacken the stem pinch bolt if you're adjusting the angle of the handlebars. If you intend to remove them fully slacken the pinch bolt or remove it completely.

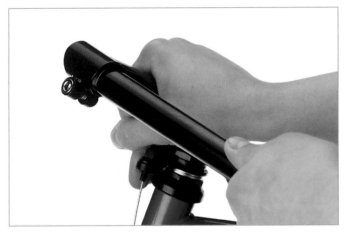

3 Apply penetrating oil and slide the bars out of the clamp. There's no need to disconnect any cables, as it's possible to remove the shifters and brakes by sliding the handlebars in the required direction.

4 If necessary the clamp can be slackened by reversing the bolt and using an old penny washer as a wedge to spread the clamp open slightly. This only works on stems with a threaded bolt-hole.

CARBON FIBRE HANDLEBARS

If you're lucky enough to have a bike fitted with carbon fibre handlebars, take care when tightening the stem clamp bolts. Use a file to remove any sharp edges from the clamp and stem.

A torque wrench with a very low torque setting (normally 5Nm) should be used to tighten the stem clamp bolts. This torque wrench is preset at 5Nm.

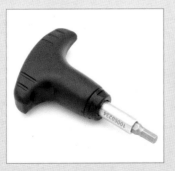

Grips and tape

Drop handlebars have traditionally been fitted with cork tape. Cork tapes are still available, but so are a wide variety of vinyl tapes. These are supplied in a multitude of colours and textures. Flat-bar bikes are fitted with grips. These are also available in a wide variety of styles, colours and textures.

Both flat bars and drop handlebars should always have bar end plugs fitted. Not only do they trap the end of the tape on drop bars and stop dirt entering the handlebars on flat-bar bikes, they're also an important safety feature. Without them the handlebars can cause serious injury in the event of a crash.

Flat-bar bikes may have bar ends fitted. These are useful for climbing, but shouldn't be used for general riding, as the brake levers aren't easily accessible. Flat and riser handlebars are available in a wide range of lengths and rises. Recent trends have seen the arrival of very wide handlebars, up to 780mm in length. These are suitable for serious off-road use, but for general riding it's possible to cut them down to a more sensible length. The bars are normally marked with cutting points.

When replacing the tape on drop handlebars thoroughly clean the bars before applying the new tape. On drop handlebars that have a groove for the brake and gear cables, use electrical tape to hold the cables in place while you apply the new handlebar tape.

Fitting new grips

1 Remove the bar end plug and then use a thin screwdriver to lift the grip. Apply some penetrating fluid to loosen the grip. If you're replacing the grips they can be cut off with a sharp knife.

2 Twist and pull the grip off. Apply more penetrating fluid if needed.

3 Clean the handlebars. A little bit of methylated spirit helps to lubricate the new grips while fitting them. Another alternative is to use hair lacquer – this acts as a lubricant, and when dry helps to stick the new grips to the handlebars.

4 Slide the new grips into position before the methylated spirit evaporates.

5 To finish the job fit new bar end plugs.

WHEN YOU NEED TO DO THIS:
- When new components need to be fitted.
- When the grips or tape are worn or damaged.

TIME:
- Ten minutes to fit new grips.
- Thirty minutes to replace drop handlebar tape.

DIFFICULTY: 🔧🔧
- Straightforward, but overlapping traditional cork bar tape can take a while to get just right.

Taping drop handlebars

1 Where fitted, loosen and pull out the bar end plugs. Some are a simple push-fit. You may have to use a screwdriver to lever this type free.

2 Unravel or cut free the old tape. Roll back the brake lever hoods. If the hoods are perished this is a good time to replace them. A short section of tape is normally supplied with the kit, to cover the side of the brake lever.

3 Start close to the centre of the handlebar, carefully overlapping the tape as you work your way to the end. When you near the end tuck the tape into the handlebar end.

BAR END CLAMPS
A wide variety of bar ends are available including carbon fibre ones. Don't over-tighten the pinch bolt as there's a slight chance you may crush the end of the handlebar. The angle of the bar is very much a personal choice but remember that they're primarily used for climbing, especially when out of the saddle.

LOCK-ON BAR GRIPS
Upgrading to lock-on grips is always worthwhile. These provide an easy way to remove and refit gear changers and brakes for overhaul or repair.

4 Fit the new bar end caps with a twisting action, trapping the end of the bar tape in the end of the handlebar as you do so.

5 Replacement bar tape is normally supplied as a complete kit with new bar end plugs, adhesive tape (to anchor the inboard end of the bar tape) and two small sections of tape to cover the brake levers.

BAR END PLUGS
A wide variety of bar end plugs are available. An essential safety feature as they prevent 'apple core' injuries.

Saddles with seat-post fixings

Saddles will always be a personal choice. You may even have to try out several styles and types before finding one you're comfortable with. Most modern saddles have fairly long rails that offer a reasonable amount of fore-and-aft adjustment. As a general rule always start with the seat post clamp set in the middle of the rails.

Most seat posts allow the saddle to be tipped up or down by large amounts to cope with the multitude of seat tube angles on the market. Many are micro-adjustable, where the angle can be altered in small increments; others have a cruder adjustment system that only allows adjustment in 2mm or 3mm steps. In both cases it's always worth removing and examining the fixing bolts for signs of corrosion. With the fixing bolts removed examine the condition of the seat rails, especially where the seat post clamp has been mounted.

Compact road frames and mountain bikes all require fairly long seat posts. Lengths of 400mm aren't uncommon on mountain bikes. Bikes fitted with interrupted or bent seat tubes may require the seat post to be cut down to suit the rider. Ideally a guide tool should be used; however, having a perfect 90° saw cut isn't essential. Before cutting the seat post note how far from the bottom the maximum height mark is and make a new mark the same distance from the bottom on the now shortened tube.

Seat posts come in many diameters. They tend to range from 25mm right through to 32.4mm, with at least five different sizes between these extremes. If there's no marking on your seat post and you wish to replace it, you'll have to measure it very carefully using Vernier calipers. If calipers aren't available, then take it with you to your local bike shop to obtain a replacement. Some manufacturers only supply one diameter of seat post and then offer a series of shims of varying thicknesses to allow the post to be fitted to any bike frame.

ADJUSTING THE SADDLE ON TWO-BOLT SEAT POSTS
This top-of-the-range seat post uses a two-clamp fixing system and has indexed marks machined into the seat post head to aid alignment and facilitate setting the saddle at the correct angle.

Adjusting I-beam saddles

1 A single hex bolt secures the saddle on the SDG I-beam system.

2 With the bolts loosened the saddle can be moved fore and aft and pitched up and down.

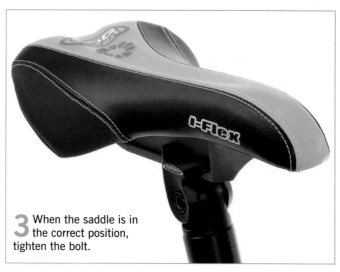

3 When the saddle is in the correct position, tighten the bolt.

Fitting the saddle

1 On this type of seat post the saddle is secured by a single bolt. Apply plenty of anti-seize compound when fitting the saddle. Single-bolt seat posts should always have the bolt checked at regular intervals.

2 It's easier to fit the saddle if this seat post is removed from the frame. Turn the saddle upside down and fit the upper clamp and pivot nut.

3 Slide the lower half of the clamp on to the saddle rails, ensuring that the cut-outs in the clamp align with the saddle rails.

4 Next fit the seat post complete with the fixing bolt. This can be a fiddly procedure, so take your time. Don't fully tighten the bolt at this stage.

Adjusting the saddle position

1 With the seat post removed, apply a liberal coating of anti-seize compound. Set the height as described in the section on setting up your bike (page 16).

2 Many saddle rails have a numerical guide printed on the side of the rail to aid alignment. Start with the seat-post clamp in the middle of the rails and with the nose of the saddle slightly raised. This is a good starting point.

3 With single-bolt seat posts, the angle of the saddle tends to change as you tighten the bolt. Don't be tempted to tap the saddle into the correct position, as this tends to ruin the serrations on the lower clamp and post head. Always slacken the fixing bolt and try again.

4 Once the saddle is correctly aligned, tighten the fixing bolt.

DROPPER POST
Dropper posts (right) mean you can change your saddle height on-the-fly. This is especially useful when descending on a mountain bike. A dropper post fits into your seat tube and has a hydraulic hose running from it. This either runs to your handlebars externally or internally. A remote lever fits to your bars where you can decide if you want to ride 'high' or 'low'.

WHEN YOU NEED TO DO THIS:
- When replacing the saddle seat post.
- When altering the riding position.

TIME:
- Three minutes to alter the position of the saddle.
- Thirty minutes to replace the saddle or seat post.

DIFFICULTY:
- Straightforward.

Saddles with clip fixing

B ikes fitted with a clip-fix seat post are to be found at the lower end of the market. The fixing itself is made of several pieces of pressed steel and a central bolt. If you do need to disassemble it then keep the parts in the correct order. The mounting bolt is normally to the rear of the seat post. However, if you want to move the saddle a little further forward it's possible to spin it round and mount the saddle with the bolt at the front of the seat post.

SEAT POST CLAMPS

The removable seat post clamp has taken over from the traditional pinch bolt. They may be of the quick release variety or they may use a hex bolt to tighten them. The diameter of the clamp is based on the outside diameter of the seat tube. The quick release clamp is favoured by mountain bikers, as they can drop the saddle height quickly for steep descents. If you fit a quick release seat post clamp to a town bike it can be a useful anti-theft measure, as you can always take the seat post and saddle with you – assuming, of course, you have the space to carry them.

SADDLE

SADDLE RAILS

SEAT POST

SADDLE CLIP

SEAT POST CLAMP

Altering the saddle height

1 On traditional bikes the saddle is locked into position with a pinch bolt. Slacken this bolt to release the seat post. If the post is reluctant to move try moving it from side to side first.

2 Turn the saddle from side to side and pull it up or push it down to alter the height. Now is a good time to remove the seat post completely and apply some anti-seize compound. Tighten the pinch bolt when the saddle is at the correct height.

WHEN YOU NEED TO DO THIS:
- When new components need to be fitted.

TIME:
- Five minutes to alter the saddle.
- Thirty minutes to an hour to replace the saddle or seat post.

DIFFICULTY: 🔧🔧🔧
- Straightforward, but the multiple parts of the clip fixing can make this a very frustrating job. Consider upgrading to a seat post-mounted clamp system if you're replacing just the seat post.

Final saddle adjustment

1 Loosen the nuts on both sides to adjust the saddle. The final position of the saddle is very much one of personal preference.

2 Don't fully loosen the nuts or it will be impossible to make fine adjustments. Use both hands to adjust the position of the saddle.

3 Slide the saddle backwards and forwards to find the most comfortable position. As a general rule start with the saddle clip in the middle of the rail, and with the nose of the saddle level with the rear.

TRADITIONAL SADDLES
Traditional sprung saddles are still available and are still quite popular. They can be mounted to either a clip-fixing seat post or a fixed-head adjustable seat post. These saddles are often leather and consequently require a little more care and attention than standard saddles. Various proprietary cleaning and proofing compounds are available and should be used on a regular basis.

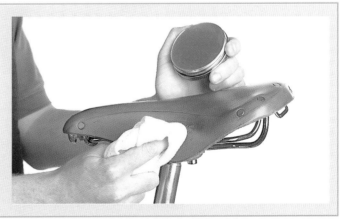

Pedals

Removal and refitting

Often overlooked, the pedals are an important contact point. At the lower end of the market, manufacturers will often fit a cheap pair of pedals, as most new buyers tend to overlook them. On high-end bikes, manufacturers are aware that keen cyclists take the issue of pedals seriously, so rarely supply them.

Cheap pedals are normally made from a hard plastic, with perhaps an alloy cage. These are such low-cost items that it's never worth stripping them and repairing them. You'll always be better advised to replace them with higher-quality ones.

For many years, traditional pedals were fitted with a toe-clip and strap. However, only an old-school traditionalist would use these today, as there are many superior systems available. For the enthusiastic road cyclist, a clipless pedal is a must. These require a specific shoe fitted with a cleat that locks the foot to the pedal. For the leisure cyclist, broad flat pedals are available, many of them supplied with replaceable metal pins that stop your feet from sliding off. These are popular with off-road riders and BMX riders.

DUST CAP

WASHER

BEARINGS

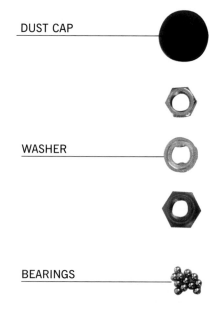

BEARINGS

RUBBER SEAL

AXLE

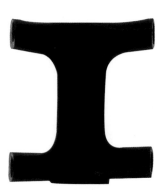

The component parts of a low-cost thermoplastic pedal. These are rarely worth repairing or overhauling due to their low price. It may be worth adjusting them and perhaps greasing them if play develops, but normally replacing them with some decent quality pedals is the best solution.

LEFT- AND RIGHT-HAND PEDALS

Pedals are normally marked with L or R, for left or right. If no marking is present it's possible to work out which pedal is which by looking closely at the threads. The thread on the left-hand pedal slopes upwards with the higher thread on the left-hand side. The opposite is true of the right-hand pedal.

Remember that the left-hand pedal has a left-hand thread and must be removed *clockwise*. The right-hand pedal has a right-hand thread and must be removed *anticlockwise*.

1 Most pedals require a 15mm pedal spanner to remove them. Some require a 17mm spanner and others have no flat provided and require a hex key to remove them. The drive-side pedal is a normal right-hand thread – unscrew *anticlockwise*.

PEDALS WITH A HEX KEY FITTING

Some modern pedals do not have a flat for use with a 15mm spanner. Instead they have a hex key fitting. A good-quality long arm hex key will be required. The best solution is a $^3/_8$th inch drive hex socket fitted with a long knuckle bar.

WHEN YOU NEED TO DO THIS:
■ When new components require fitting.

TIME:
■ Five minutes.

DIFFICULTY:
■ Straightforward, if you remember the correct direction.

2 Pedals can be notoriously difficult to remove so apply plenty of penetrating oil and allow it to soak in.

3 There's always a danger of slipping with the spanner and injuring yourself on the chainrings. As a precaution, shift the chain onto the largest chainring. Protect the chainrings with a cloth.

4 The left-hand pedal has a left-hand thread and must be loosened in a *clockwise* direction.

5 With the pedals removed, clean and inspect the threads and then apply an anti-seize compound or grease before refitting.

Pedals: strip, grease and reassemble

The quality of the pedal fitted to your bike will dictate whether it's worth repairing, servicing or simply replacing. Low-cost thermoplastic pedals will have a loose bearing fitted, while quality pedals will have cartridge bearings at the inboard end and a bush at the outboard end. Some pedals will have cartridge bearings at both ends of the axle, while others may have bushes at both ends. High-end pedals may be machined out of a single billet of aluminium and have a titanium axle.

Here we look at the overhaul of a cheap thermoplastic pedal not because it's worth doing, but because it's a suitable project for inexperienced bicycle mechanics. If you're capable of stripping, cleaning and rebuilding one of these pedals then you can consider yourself well on the road to becoming a very competent bicycle mechanic. The advantage of this exercise is that if you fail to reassemble the pedal, all is not lost, as the pedal can be replaced at very reasonable cost.

One other point to consider when contemplating overhauling a pair of pedals is the cost of any special tools required. Some Shimano pedals require tools that cost well in excess of the cost of a replacement pair of pedals.

WHEN YOU NEED TO DO THIS:
☐ When the bearings are worn.

TIME:
☐ An hour to replace the bearings on cheap thermoplastic pedals.

DIFFICULTY: 🔧🔧
☐ Other than for the practice, it will never be worth replacing bearings in cheap pedals. It's better to fit new ones.

Loose bearing pedals

1 Where possible, remove the cage from the pedal body.

2 Prise free the dust cap from the end of the pedal body. Some are recessed into the pedal, others may require unscrewing.

3 Where the lock nut is recessed into the pedal body a socket will be required to loosen it.

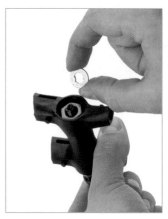

4 Remove the lock nut and lift off the tab washer. A small magnet can be used to recover the tab washer.

5 Hold the spindle and pedal body together and then remove the cone nut. Alternatively mount the pedal in a vice.

6 Remove the bearings with a suitable pick. Here we're using a pen top to remove the loose bearings.

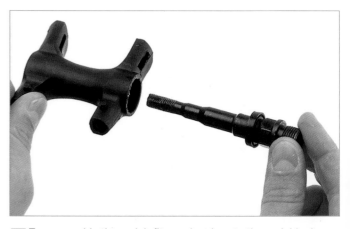

7 To reassemble the pedal, fit new bearings to the pedal body. Use a little grease to hold the bearings in place. Next carefully fit the axle into the pedal body. Refit the cone nut, tab washer and lock nut. Bearing adjustment is exactly the same as adjusting wheel bearings – see page 150.

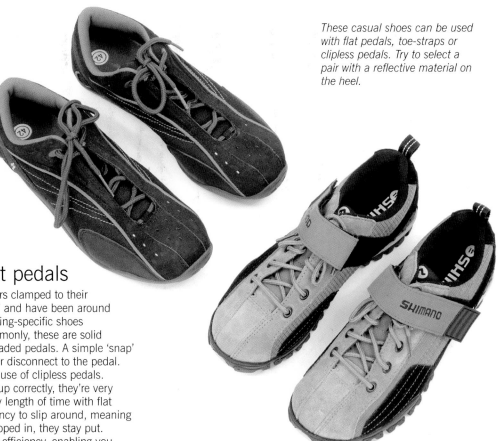

These casual shoes can be used with flat pedals, toe-straps or clipless pedals. Try to select a pair with a reflective material on the heel.

CARTRIDGE BEARING PEDALS

Quality cartridge bearing pedals can often be overhauled at a relatively low cost. This service and repair kit contains all you need to completely refurbish a pair of pedals.

Clipless pedals and flat pedals

Scan the cycle path and you'll notice riders clamped to their pedals. These are termed 'clipless pedals' and have been around since the late Eighties. They work by cycling-specific shoes connecting to your pedals by cleats. Commonly, these are solid sections of plastic that attach to spring-loaded pedals. A simple 'snap' of the ankle helps you to either connect or disconnect to the pedal.

There are two primary reasons for the use of clipless pedals. The first is that, as long as you set them up correctly, they're very comfortable. Anyone who's ridden for any length of time with flat pedals knows that your feet have a tendency to slip around, meaning constant repositioning. If your feet are clipped in, they stay put.

Clipless pedals also improve pedalling efficiency, enabling you to pull up, pull back and push forward during a pedal stroke, rather than just pull down. A correctly positioned cleat also ensures the foot is locked into the most efficient pedalling position and the solid nature of the sole of a clipless shoe means more of the rider's effort is transferred to the pedal. There are many on the market but Look, Shimano and Time are the main players. They're used for road and mountain bikes, though many who ride off-road prefer flats…

Flats are, as the name suggests, just that – flat sections of plastic or metal where your feet are free to move around and the sole of your shoes can be flat. The quality of these varies wildly, as does the size. Increasingly in mountain biking, flats are pretty large to provide a sizeable platform to increase shoe contact for more stability and control – both desirable traits when riding off-road. They also have pins rising out of them to, again, increase grip and control.

This Crank Brothers 'egg beater' pedal is suitable for both on- and off-road use. The open design sheds mud easily when used off-road.

Where possible always fit pedal reflectors. The rotation of the pedal easily catches the light from passing car headlamps. Many are a simple push-fit; the better quality ones are often bolted into place. Check the security of the bolt securing the reflector occasionally.

Clipless pedals (MTB)

1 Shoes suitable for clipless pedals will have a removable plate fitted when new. Remove the plate to access the mounting screws. On some shoes you may have to use a sharp knife to cut the sole to access the cleat-mounting screw holes.

2 With the mounting holes now exposed in the sole, align the cleat with the holes. It's generally accepted that the pedal axle should sit just behind the ball of your foot when clipped in.

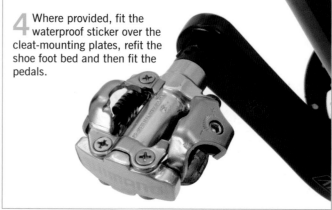

4 Where provided, fit the waterproof sticker over the cleat-mounting plates, refit the shoe foot bed and then fit the pedals.

3 If necessary, remove the foot bed from the shoe so that the mounting plate can be held in position. Fit the cleat, having smeared the threads of the mounting bolts in anti-seize compound first.

5 Many pedals have adjustable spring tension. If you're new to clipless pedals, always set the tension to minimum to start with.

6 Sit on the bike and, leaning against a wall, practise clipping and unclipping from the pedal. Adjust the position of the cleat if necessary.

Fitting cleats (road shoes)

1 Look is one of the more popular styles of clipless pedals for roadies. Like all pedals, screw them by hand into your crank arm in an anti-clockwise fashion before tightening with a spanner.

2 Many clipless pedals feature what's called 'float', which is the amount your foot can move in the pedal before release. With this pair, you can adjust the degree of float with an Allen key.

3 The sole of a road shoe is generally stiffer than a mountain-bike version. Neutral-position guides help you to align the cleat.

4 Place the cleat over the ball of the shoe so that the shoe holes are centred. Place the bolt and washer over the top hole.

5 When you're happy with the cleat alignment, screw in the first bolt, being careful not to let the cleat move. But don't tighten just yet.

6 Screw in the remaining bolts and washers, again ensuring the cleat remains in position.

7 When happy with the cleat position, tighten each of the screws. Cleat position is vital for injury-free pedalling. Everyone is different so you may have to play around with cleat position.

CLEAT POSITIONING

To assess your best cleat position, sit on a bench or chair with your feet dangling. Let your legs and feet relax. Now look at your feet. Some people's feet naturally have their heels further together and their toes slightly outward, others are the reverse or neutral.

Now with the cleat bolts loose enough so you can move the cleat, but tight enough so that they stay where they are, position the shoe by grabbing the cleat with your hand as if it were the pedal. Now position the shoe so it mimics your natural foot position. Then tighten the cleat bolts and see how it feels when clipped in.

Note: ALWAYS tighten the cleat bolts fully before clipping in otherwise the shoe can become stuck in the pedal and you may damage the shoe, the cleat and/or the pedal trying to remove them.

CHAPTER

WHEELS

Stripping down hubs

A pre-ride inspection is probably the first time that you'll notice that the hubs require attention. On old-style hubs with little or no sealing this may be more often than you think, especially if the bike has frequently been ridden in the rain or off-road.

Mountain bikes and an increasing number of road bikes have a rubber seal fitted. Though these provide a pretty good barrier against the ingress of water and grime they're not totally sealed, and will still require a strip down and overhaul occasionally. If you have a low-cost wheel with no seal then consider the cost of a replacement before overhauling it. This is always a consideration, especially if the rim is worn or damaged. However, quality hubs will always be worth overhauling and adjusting.

Increasingly hubs with cartridge bearings are being fitted to quality wheel sets. Only Shimano and Campagnolo seem to be persisting with loose-bearing hubs. They say it's down to loose cup-and-cone hubs handling sideway loads better, which ultimately means they can retain more speed through corners. The overhaul and replacement of cartridge bearing wheels is shown on pages 152–153.

Recent developments have seen the introduction of complete wheel sets by hub manufacturers. These may be fitted with standard spokes or specialist spokes that dispense with the nipple at the rim. Some have straight-pull spokes with the tension adjustment nipple now at the hub.

On rear hubs that have a freehub body, the axle and bearings will have to be removed before the freehub can be. On rear hubs fitted with cartridge bearings this isn't normally required, as the freehub is a push-fit on to the main hub shell.

GREASE FOR HUB BEARINGS
There are many bike-specific grease formulations on the market. These are often synthetic compounds with added Teflon. They have a viscosity suited to the relatively low rpm bicycle wheel. Automotive greases aren't really suitable, but could be used if nothing else is available.

WHEN YOU NEED TO DO THIS:
☐ When play develops in the wheel.
☐ When the bearings feel rough or noisy.

TIME:
☐ Allow 45 minutes to an hour to replace the bearings, longer if you're also replacing the axle and cones.

DIFFICULTY: ✎✎✎✎
☐ It can be quite time-consuming to eliminate the play from adjustable bearings.

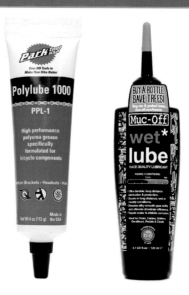

QUICK-RELEASE LEVER

QUICK-RELEASE SKEWER

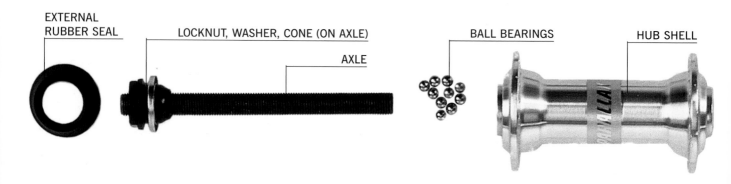

EXTERNAL RUBBER SEAL

LOCKNUT, WASHER, CONE (ON AXLE)

AXLE

BALL BEARINGS

HUB SHELL

Stripping down a hub

1 With the wheel removed from the bike, fully remove the quick release. Note the orientation of the volute spring – the narrow end of the spring faces towards the hub.

2 Many hubs now feature a rubber seal to prevent the ingress of water. Use a small screwdriver to unpick the seal or simply pull it off.

3 Use a cone spanner and a standard spanner to remove the lock nut from the axle.

4 Remove the lock nut and recover any washer fitted below it. Next unthread the cone nut.

5 With the cone and lock nut removed from one side, pull out the axle. You may find that some of the ball bearings come out as the axle is removed. You need to collect these.

6 Using a small pick or screwdriver, collect any ball bearings left in the hub.

RIMS

This is high-quality double-wall rim with reinforced eyelets to support the spoke nipples. The use of this type of quality rim is limited to mid- and upper-price-range bikes.

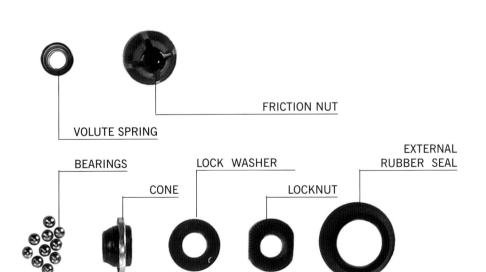

VOLUTE SPRING

FRICTION NUT

BEARINGS

CONE

LOCK WASHER

LOCKNUT

EXTERNAL RUBBER SEAL

REMOVING A FREEHUB BODY

After removing the axle and bearings the freehub body can then be removed from the hub shell. Shimano freehub bodies aren't serviceable – if faulty or worn, they must be replaced.

Greasing and adjusting hubs

With the hub apart and stripped down, thoroughly clean and then inspect all the component parts. First check that the axle isn't bent. This is easy to do by rolling it up and down a flat surface – a sheet of glass is ideal. Next check the condition of the bearing cones. Grooves and pitting of the surface will mean that the cones require replacing. Finally examine the bearing seats in the hub. Any damage here will require the replacement of the complete hub, as very few manufacturers supply replacement seats.

With the hub reassembled, using new parts where required, the preload on the bearings must be adjusted. Tighten the cone against the bearings so that there's no perceptible movement in the axle. The wheel must be free to turn, with no tight spots and no play. With a cone spanner on the cone, tighten up the lock nut with a suitable spanner. This procedure can often be time-consuming and will require a little bit of trial and error to find the sweet spot, where the wheel spins freely with no play at the rim.

PITTED CONES
Inspect the old cones for wear and pitting. Compare the new cone (left) shown above with the two worn ones. The middle cone is pitted and rusty and should be replaced immediately. The cone on the right is worn and should also be replaced.

1 Having thoroughly cleaned the hub, apply grease to the circumference of the bearing seat. Don't apply an excessive amount.

2 Next fit new ball bearings into the hub. The grease will hold them in place. Use a pen top or cocktail stick to place them in the hub. Most hubs require between 9 and 11 bearings per side.

3 Grease the cone and then carefully refit the axle.

4 Carefully screw on the cone nut and adjust it against the bearings so that there's no perceptible play.

DISC BRAKE HUB
This hub has a six-bolt mounting for a disc brake. This is the international standard mounting, but note that Shimano use their own centre lock mounting system for fitting a disc rotor.

5 Fit the washer and lock nut. Thread the lock nut up against the cone nut.

6 Hold the cone nut steady with the cone spanner and tighten up the lock nut. Check that the wheel rotates freely with no play at the axle.

7 It may take several attempts to eliminate the play from the hub and get the wheel running just so. Refit the wheel and test ride the bike. Further adjustment may be necessary after the test ride.

NEW AXLE
When fitting a new axle and cones the amount of exposed thread outside the lock nut is crucial. Use the position of the lock nut on the old axle to determine the position of the lock nut on the new axle. This is important to ensure that there's sufficient support for the axle in the dropouts.

WHEN YOU NEED TO DO THIS:
■ When play develops in the wheel.

TIME:
■ Allow 15 minutes to adjust the bearings.

DIFFICULTY:
■ Eliminating the play from adjustable bearings can be quite time-consuming.

Cartridge-bearing hubs

Whilst Shimano and Campagnolo continue with loose-bearing or caged-bearing hubs, many other manufacturers have adopted cartridge bearings. These are normally single-row sealed bearings. Further sealing may also be built into the hub. These bearings should be considered non-adjustable. Where adjustment is provided this is used to lock the axle in position – it isn't designed to remove any play from the bearings.

Cartridge-bearing hubs are normally found on mid- to high-end bikes, often as part of a complete wheel set. Perhaps the biggest advantage of hubs featuring cartridge bearings is that they tend to all take standard bearings that are widely available. A full range of other parts such as spacers and axles is also normally available from the same manufacturer. Other advantages are that they're often very adaptable to suit the many axle standards now available. The Hope

front hub set can be used with a 20mm bolt-through downhill axle, the newer 15mm standard and the traditional quick release 9mm standard. One other advantage is that rear-wheel cartridge bearing hubs will normally have a freehub body that's user-serviceable and if required repairable.

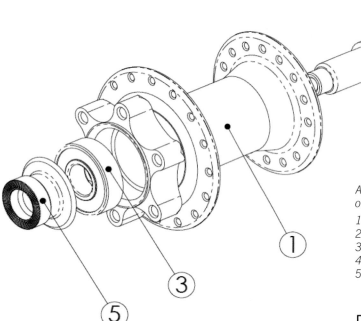

All parts are available to fully overhaul this Hope front hub.

1 Hub
2 Axle
3 Bearing
4 End cap (7mm)
5 End cap (13mm)

WHEN YOU NEED TO DO THIS:
■ When play develops in the wheel.
■ When the bearings feel rough or noisy.

TIME:
■ Allow 45 minutes to an hour to replace the bearings.

DIFFICULTY:
■ Straightforward if you have a suitable collection of old sockets. We used a suitably drilled piece of old oak floorboard to construct a jig to help with removing the bearings.

Replacing cartridge bearings

1 Cover the hub and spokes with a soft cloth and then lever off the end-caps from the hub on both sides.

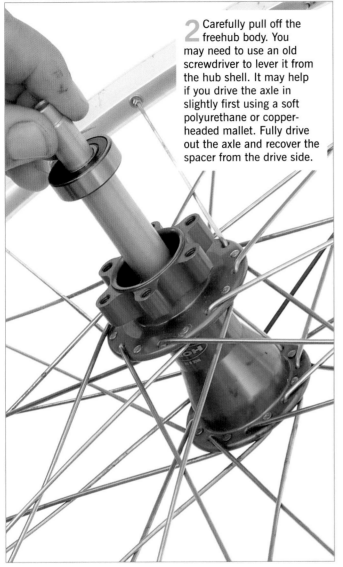

2 Carefully pull off the freehub body. You may need to use an old screwdriver to lever it from the hub shell. It may help if you drive the axle in slightly first using a soft polyurethane or copper-headed mallet. Fully drive out the axle and recover the spacer from the drive side.

3 Recover the three small springs and pawls from the freehub body or the hub shell. Within the freehub body there's a small spacer. Move this to one side with a punch and then drive out the bearing. Remove the circlip and drive the other bearing from the freehub body.

4 Use a suitable socket to fit the replacement bearings to the freehub body. Align the internal freehub body spacer using a round bar or screwdriver.

5 Using suitable old sockets that bear only on the outer race of the bearing, drive in the new bearings squarely and evenly.

6 Refit the axle, remembering to fit the spacer to the drive side. Apply grease to the hub body drive-side ratchet surface.

7 Thoroughly clean the freehub body and examine the springs and pawls for wear or damage, replacing any that look in poor condition. Locate the springs and ratchet pawls correctly in the slots in the freehub body.

8 We used a tie wrap to locate and retain the pawls in their correct positions and then dropped the freehub body into the hub. As soon as the pawls engaged we used a sharp knife to cut free the tie wrap. Check the ratchet mechanism for smooth operation and then refit the end-caps.

Simple wheel truing and spoke replacement

The full strength of a wheel is dependent on all the spokes being equally and correctly tensioned. A broken or loose spoke will severely compromise the strength of the wheel. Good-quality rims can often cope with a loose or broken spoke, but cheap rims will often suffer permanent damage.

Most off-the-shelf wheels are built in a factory by a machine, whereas custom wheels will be hand-built to your specification. Specialist wheels that don't use the traditional spoke lacing pattern are often part machine-built and then finished by hand in the factory. If you're replacing a damaged or worn-out wheel there's a large range of replacement wheels to choose from. There's little point in fitting a custom wheelset to a simple basic steel bike frame. On the other hand if you have a decent-quality frame then consider a custom wheelset built to your own specifications. Your local bike shop will be able to advise you on the best option for your particular type of riding.

Traditional wheels are trued and tensioned by nipples located at the rim. These square-sided nipples come in a variety of sizes. It's important that you have the right size spanner, universally referred to as a 'spoke key'. By turning the nipple at the rim the tension on the spoke can be increased or decreased as required. If the nipple won't turn apply plenty of penetrating fluid. It may be necessary to remove the tyre, tube and rim tape to apply penetrating oil to the head of the nipple, but if you're replacing a broken spoke you'll have to do this anyway.

Wheel building and wheel truing are often described as the 'black arts' of the bicycle world. In reality there's no mystery involved in the process, just a little bit of patience and logical thinking. The most common mistake beginners make is to tighten an individual spoke far too much in relation to its neighbours on the same side of the hub. Unless a spoke is excessively loose then turn the nipple on each spoke no more then half a revolution at a time. As the spoke on one side is tightened, the corresponding spoke on the other side of the hub should be slackened.

SPOKE BREAKDOWN

There are various types of spokes (straight-pull, aerodynamic and more) and ways of lacing spokes, with each down to six basic considerations: strength, flexibility, torque resistance, air resistance, weight and aesthetic. Strength, for instance, is dictated by the number of spokes, how they're arranged, and how they interface with the hub and rim. Probably the most common lacing system is a three-cross, 32-hole hub and rim combination. This has more lines of symmetry than any other combination, meaning each spoke is supported by another spoke and so results in a strong, stiff wheel. Another common lacing arrangement is known as 'radial', and is often used by riders seeking an aerodynamic advantage or weight saving. Hence, these are popular with roadies. This is where the spokes leave the hub at right angles to the circumference. With radially laced wheels, you'll often see the spokes reversed, with the nipples on the hub end because the hub must be redesigned to stand the stress. Be aware that radial-laced wheels are stiffer against radial forces, but critics argue that they don't resist torque force very well so aren't ideal when using disc brakes.

Fitting a new spoke

1 Spokes usually break close to the hub or by the nipple. If you're working on the drive-side of the rear wheel you'll have to remove the cassette first. On bikes fitted with disc brakes you may have to remove the disc if the broken spoke is on the disc brake side of the hub.

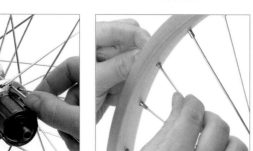

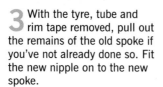

2 Using the next but one spoke as a guide, fit the new spoke. You'll need to flex the spoke gently to fit it through the hub and weave it between the other spokes.

3 With the tyre, tube and rim tape removed, pull out the remains of the old spoke if you've not already done so. Fit the new nipple on to the new spoke.

4 A screwdriver can be used to take up the slack; then use a spoke key for final adjustment.

5 Pluck the other spokes in the wheel to get an idea of the correct tension and then tighten up the new spoke nipple. Next follow the procedure for truing a wheel.

REPLACING A DAMAGED RIM

Whilst not an ideal solution, it's possible to replace a badly damaged rim by simply slackening off all the spokes in the old wheel and taping on a new rim. However, note that at the very least you should replace every spoke nipple.

With the new rim securely taped or tie wrapped to the old wheel, swap the spokes over one at a time. With all the spokes swapped over, remove the damaged rim and true-up the rebuilt wheel.

HOME-MADE WHEEL-BUILDING JIG

It's possible for a competent home mechanic to build their own wheel-truing jig. This home-made jig was simply constructed in an afternoon, and whilst perhaps not as accurate as a professional wheel builder's jig it's perfectly functional.

Another simple solution is to use the bike frame itself as a jig. A pencil can be secured to the frame to act as a guide for wheel truing.

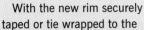

SPOKE LENGTHS

Spokes come in a variety of lengths. The easiest way to obtain the correct replacement is to remove a spoke from the opposite side of the hub, but from the same side of the hub on rear wheels as most rear wheels are offset to one side of the hub to allow for fitting of the rear sprockets. Take the spoke with you to your local bike shop to obtain an exact replacement. Alternatively a spoke ruler can be used to measure the length required.

Truing a wheel

1 Fit the wheel in the frame or home-made jig and slowly rotate it until you've located the out-of-true section. Use a pencil to mark this section if necessary.

2 If the wheel moves to the right then tension the spokes on the left-hand side and slacken the spokes on the right-hand side. Remember to always work on groups of spokes, not individual spokes.

WHEN YOU NEED TO DO THIS:

■ When a spoke breaks.
■ When the wheel is running out of true.

TIME:

■ Allow 15 minutes to an hour to replace a single spoke.
■ One to two hours if you're swapping a rim over, especially if it's the first time you've done it.

DIFFICULTY: 🔧🔧🔧🔧🔧

■ Patience is the key to successfully truing wheels and replacing spokes. Very difficult to get right the first time, but it does get easier with practice.

3 A little goes a long way when it comes to wheel truing. Always make small micro adjustments to groups of spokes to true the wheel correctly.

4 When you've finished, apply some tension to each pair of spokes to de-stress them. Finally, roll the wheel along the ground, applying pressure to the rim as you rotate it. This will fully relieve any stress in the spokes.

7

CHAPTER

FRAMES, FORKS, STEERING AND SUSPENSION

Frame materials and design

For many years, simple steel-framed bikes were those most commonly available. Bottom-of-the-range bikes were often made of plain gauge steel tubing with perhaps some chromium added. Middle- and top-of-the-range bikes would use exotic steel tubes often referred to as butted tubes. On a butted tube, the wall thickness varies internally. This process was developed by Reynolds, and the name Reynolds has become synonymous with steel tubing. These tubes are often referred to as Reynolds 531 or 953, for example. Reynolds and Columbus (another popular manufacturer of steel tubes) are still widely available and are a popular choice for custom-built frames.

Steel bikes traditionally had their tubes joined together by a series of lugs – preformed brackets into which the steel tubes could be fitted and brazed together to form a complete bicycle. Today cheap steel-framed bikes are simply welded together, but custom-built bikes will still use traditional lugs to join the main frame tubes.

Aluminium is now the most common material for the majority of affordable bicycle frames. Aluminium bikes may be built of simple extruded aluminium alloy tubes or heavily manipulated and butted exotic aluminium alloys. To achieve the many complex and convoluted shapes of mid- to high-end bikes the aluminium tubes are often hydro-formed. This is a process whereby a basic tube shape is forced under intense hydraulic pressure into the complex shape of a mould. Aluminium-framed bicycle tubes are joined together by TIG (tungsten inert gas) welding.

Top-of-the-range bike frames may well be made out of steel or aluminium, but carbon fibre and, to a certain extent, titanium has increasingly become the material of choice for top-end models. Incredibly strong for a given weight, carbon-fibre frames are very light and very stiff, and why the world's best road-race teams, like Sky, use Pinarello carbon bikes. The frames may be made from a selection of carbon-fibre tubes bonded together or, increasingly, as a complete bicycle frame made in a one-piece mould. Most carbon-fibre frames have steel or aluminium fittings bonded into the frame to allow the mounting of bicycle hardware.

Titanium-framed bikes are very much at the top end of the market, strictly reserved for discerning cyclists who know exactly what they require from a frame. Correctly designed they can have the compliance of a steel-framed bicycle and the stiffness of an aluminium frame.

As the materials that bicycle frames are made out of has changed over the years, so too has their shape and design. Traditional frames have evolved from the classic double-triangle frame with its horizontal top tube to the compact triangle of the modern road bike. Step-through bikes have dispensed with the top tube completely, and mountain bikes, especially full-suspension ones, have developed complicated and convoluted frame designs. This has all been made possible by the application of CAD (computer-aided design) software and modern manufacturing techniques.

Perhaps the most innovative design of recent years has been the adoption of suspension forks for many bicycles coupled with the abandonment on many mid-range bikes of the traditional threaded fork-steerer type in favour of threadless steerers. Suspension forks have become essential items on many mountain bikes and have also found a home on commuter bikes. The threadless steerer, commonly known as an Aheadset, has reduced production costs and simplified adjustment. It also provides an easy method of customising your riding position.

This hybrid city bike has heavy-duty 700c wheels and a simple aluminium frame, while hydraulic disc brakes ensure low maintenance. The upright riding position is ideal for urban commuting.

This hard-tail mountain bike has the main frame constructed from several hydro-formed tubes. It has hydraulic disc brakes and the latest ten-speed Sram X7 groupset. It's eminently suitable for serious off-road use.

Design features

1 This mountain bike has extra plates (often known as gussets) welded to the head tube to reinforce the connection between head tube, top tube and down tube. Any serious impact damage will often show up here as a ripple just behind the head tube.

2 Standards have changed over time. This is an oversize head tube fitted with an integrated headset. On this system the headset bearings are mounted directly inside the head tube.

3 This mountain bike has seat stays that curl in to allow the mounting of brakes and then curl out again to allow the fitting of a large-volume tyre.

4 On this bike you can see clearly the TIG-welded frame. Note also the easily accessible cable stops.

5 This road bike has carbon fibre forks fitted. They're light and stiff, but have enough compliance built into them to filter out any harsh road shocks or vibrations.

6 Most quality frames now feature a replaceable gear hanger. These have a weak point built into them just above the derailleur mounting bolt. In the event of a crash the hanger will break free from the frame, leaving the frame undamaged (in theory).

7 This bike has hydro-formed tubes. Hydro-forming allows complex frame tubes to be produced that vary in both shape and wall thickness throughout their length.

8 This classic lug-framed steel bike has brazed-on fittings for mudguards, a rack and bicycle pump.

This racing bike has a full carbon fibre frame and forks. Carbon fibre provides an extremely light and stiff frame. By varying the thickness and direction of the carbon fibre cloth, strength and rigidity can be designed into the frame at the appropriate points.

This touring bike features a traditional Reynolds 631 lugged and butted steel frame. Extensive brazed-on fittings allow the addition of a front and rear pannier rack. Two bottle cage mounts are also fitted.

Safety inspection

If you're buying a new bike, the condition and alignment of the frame shouldn't be an issue. However, it's not unknown for new bikes to be supplied with a misaligned or twisted frame, so it's always worth giving any frame, new or second-hand, a visual once-over. On traditional triangle-framed bikes it's quite easy to check the alignment by simply eyeballing the frame from the front and rear. On newer frames with curved and bent tubes that change shape throughout their length it's not so easy.

If you're buying a second-hand bike, take your time to thoroughly inspect the frame. Pay particular attention to the top tube and down tube immediately behind the head tube, as this is where most impact damage shows itself. Next, examine the bottom-bracket shell area, especially the drive-side chain stay as this is where fatigue cracks can often occur due to the loading of the frame on the drive side.

At the front, check the alignment of the forks, paying particular attention to where the fork blades meet the fork crown. Any front impact damage will often show up as cracked paintwork in this area. Finally, run your hands all over the frame, feeling for any irregularities and cracks in the paintwork. Your fingers are very sensitive and can often feel damage that the eye can't see. In many ways it's better to spend your time checking out the frame on a second-hand bike rather than any of the components. An overlooked worn derailleur can be easily replaced; however, a cracked or twisted frame will rarely be worth replacing on a second-hand bike.

When buying a new bike or frame, ask the retailer about the terms of the warranty. Some manufacturers will offer a lifetime warranty to the original purchaser. Many, however, have a limited warranty that may be as little as three years. One or two manufacturers do offer a limited transferable warranty. While in the shop, also ask about the manufacturer's crash replacement policy, as many will often supply a discounted new frame in the event of the bike frame being damaged in a crash or an accident.

CRASH DAMAGE
This frame has obvious impact damage to the top tube just behind the head tube. This is a classic place for damage to occur in a head-on crash.

The crack in the second picture will be hard to spot as it's in an unusual place, and whereas most welds will crack next to the weld this frame has a crack down the centre of the weld.

REAR HANGER
Although it's sometimes possible to straighten a bent hanger, you're better off replacing it. A website like wheelsmfg.com will guide you to the specific hanger for your bike.

1 Remove the rear derailleur from the hanger with a 5mm Allen key or T25 torx key. Some bikes have a button or lever that releases tension in the chain. Make sure this is pressed or shifted.

2 Just let your rear derailleur hang loosely from the rear of your frame and then remove the rear wheel.

3 Unscrew the existing hanger with an Allen key. This varies between 2mm and 6mm. Hold onto the bolt, although your replacement hanger should come with a new bolt.

4 When fitting the replacement, the correct hanger should naturally slip into the frame. Then simply reverse the process until your rear derailleur's screwed back on and your wheel's refitted.

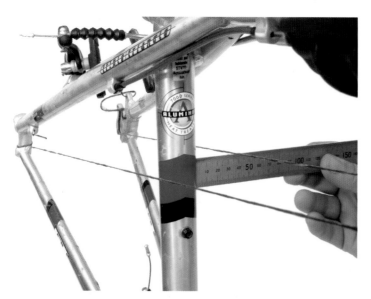

CHECKING FRAME ALIGNMENT
Special tools are available to check frame alignment. However, a length of string, a ruler and a plumb line can be used to assess the alignment of most frames. Run stout string from the rear drop outs and up and around the head tube and then use a ruler to make sure that the seat tube sits perfectly in the middle of the string lines.

FRAME TUBING

With popular aluminium tube sets, such as the 7005 series, zinc and magnesium are added to the base alloy. Frames are often referred to as 'alloy' or 'steel'– these are just general classifications. A steel frame is rarely pure steel, as most contain other metals to produce a durable frame-building material. For example, most steel frame tube sets will contain varying amounts of chromium, nickel, manganese and vanadium. Here are the three big cycling steel manufacturers and a sample of their respective ranges...

Columbus

Niobium – special steel containing manganese, chrome, nickel, molybdenum and niobium.
XCR – jewel in the Columbus crown, employs triple- and double-butted tubing.
Nemo – length and proportions of tubing designed for stiffness.

Reynolds

525 – an entry-level butted steel tube for brazing and welding.
725 – a low carbon chromium and molybdenum double-butted steel tube.
853 – a high-end steel alloy tube containing carbon, manganese, silicon, and copper.
953 – a top of the range steel alloy containing chromium, nickel, manganese and titanium.

Dedacciai

Series Zero – a low carbon chromium heat-treated tempered steel alloy.
D7.9 – a top-of-the-range hydro-formed and heat-treated aluminium alloy.

CARBON FIBRE

In recent years carbon fibre-framed bikes have become widely available at the top end of the market. Whilst the frames are incredibly tough and resilient, they can be damaged or suffer from catastrophic failure, especially if impacted from the side. That's because the fibres run unilaterally. Any frame that's been in an accident or been dropped should be inspected thoroughly for any damage. Assessing damage to a carbon fibre frame is a job for an expert. Cracks in the surface may just be minor surface damage, but may also be indicative of underlying terminal damage. The advice of an expert should be sought if there's any doubt as to the extent of the damage.

TITANIUM

Up there with carbon fibre frames when it comes to its exotic nature, titanium-framed bikes are renowned for their durability and fatigue strength. They're always constructed from a titanium alloy often referred to as 3AL-2.5v, which contains approximately 3% aluminium and 2.5% vanadium. Most frames are left unpainted or have a coat of clear lacquer.

Checking for crash damage

1 Position yourself at the front of the bike, squat down and look along the frame. You should be able to see if the head tube and the seat tube that carries the saddle line up.

2 Stand over the bike looking down. You'll be able to see if the horizontal top tube lines up with the diagonal down tube. Also check that the forks splay out an equal amount.

3 Now look along the frame from the back. The rear mech should hang down straight and the seat tube should align with the head tube. Make sure also that the seat stays are straight and undamaged.

4 Run your fingers down the back and front of the forks, checking for ripples in the tubing. Check also that the fork curves look smooth, and drop the front wheel out so that you can see if it fits back in easily.

Headset removal, replacement and adjustment

To enable the front wheel to steer, all bicycles are fitted with a bearing assembly in the head tube of the frame. From the original 1in standard right through to the latest 1.5 tapered head tube standard, they all rely on bearings at the top and bottom of the head tube. Traditionally the steerer tube from the fork was threaded and two large diameter nuts were fitted. By adjusting the nuts and using the second nut to lock the first in position, play in the bearings could be eliminated. This system is still fitted to many older and low-cost bikes. However, the majority of new bikes are now fitted with a threadless steerer instead, commonly referred to as an Aheadset or 'A'-head. This confusing name applies to the original threadless steerer system developed and patented by Dia Compe (now Cane Creek).

The threadless 'A'-head system has many advantages, the most notable being simple and easy adjustment of any play in the headset bearings. Manufacturing costs are also reduced and the ease of swapping stems allows the rider to easily customise the handlebar position to suit their own particular style of riding.

Most headsets still have traditional external bearing cups that retain either loose bearings, caged bearings or cartridge bearings. Recent developments have seen the introduction of integral, integrated, tapered and oversize headsets. Integral headsets have traditional bearing cups that fit inside the larger diameter head tube. Integrated headsets have the cartridge bearings sitting directly into the head tube. Tapered headsets, as their name suggests, have a larger diameter bearing at the bottom of the head tube and a standard $1^1/8$ headset bearing at the top. The lower bearing is often described as oversize or 1.5in. A special fork with a tapered steerer is required for these. Adaptors are available to allow the fitting of a standard fork.

Oversize headsets are often called 1.5 headsets. These feature larger bearings and will accommodate either a standard fork or one fitted with a tapered steerer.

Regardless of which system is fitted, the principal of removing the bearings and fitting new ones is the same, except for the integrated headset where the bearings sit directly in the head tube. On all the other systems, the bearing cups must be driven out of the head tube and new ones pressed into place.

STEM CAP

COMPRESSION BOLT

STAR NUT

CLAMP BOLT

SPACERS

TOP BEARING RACE

BOTTOM BEARING RACE

CROWN RACE

WHEN YOU NEED TO DO THIS:
■ During a major overhaul.
■ When play develops in the steering.

TIME:
■ Allow an hour to strip out and replace headset bearings.

DIFFICULTY: 🔧🔧🔧
■ Whilst not difficult, adjusting the bearings on a traditional threaded steerer system can be quite time-consuming.

Removing headset bearing cups

1 Secure the forks to the down tube with a tie wrap and then remove the stem. Secure the handlebars and stem to the top tube with another tie wrap. Disconnect the brake cable from the lever or remove the caliper from the fork.

2 Recover any spacers and then remove the top cap to access the conical washer. If the washer is hard to remove wait until the forks have been lowered and removed.

3 Cut off the tie wrap and lower the forks from the frame. Remove the lower bearing from the fork crown and inspect it.

4 A headset press, like that used on page 115, is a good option here. However, some mechanics are still happy to use a length of copper pipe to drive the bearing cup from the head tube.

5 Inspect the head tube, bearings and bearing cups and then refit the cups. We used a length of threaded bar and some large aluminium washers to refit them.

6 Although not ideal, if a length of threaded bar and suitable washers or sockets aren't available, the cups can also be driven home using a block of wood.

7 To remove the bearing seats from the forks a specialist crown race puller can be used. Note, however, that many newer headsets often have a split crown race that can easily be lifted from the crown race seat.

8 If you don't have the specialist tool, work around the base of the crown race with the blade of a knife and a small hammer until a gap appears, then use a cold chisel to ease off.

CAGED BEARINGS
Caged bearings are one step up from loose bearings. They're easy to clean and inspect. If the bearings (and more importantly the bearing seats) are in good condition then re-grease and refit them. New caged bearings are widely available and it's even possible to pop the individual bearings out of the cage and simply replace them.

Replacing and adjusting threadless headset bearings

1 Remove the top cap bolt and then loosen the stem pinch bolts.

2 Lift off the stem and recover any spacing washers fitted. The compression ring will normally hold the forks in place.

3 Tap down the forks and then push them up to recover the compression ring. Alternatively you can lift the ring up with a screwdriver or sharp knife.

4 Slide up the compression ring and recover the upper cartridge bearing cover. Some types of headset may have further washers fitted above the bearing.

5 Now carefully remove the forks from the frame. Clean and inspect the forks, the bearings and the head tube.

6 If the bearings are in good condition, clean them and then re-grease them. Fit the lower bearing to the fork crown.

7 Refit the forks and slide on the bearings, washers and compression ring. Fit the spacers and then refit the stem.

8 Refit the top cap bolt. Note that on the ahead system the steerer tube must be slightly below the stem to allow the top cap to adjust the bearings.

9 Tighten the top cap bolt until there's no play present in the headset. Pull the front brake on and rock the bike backwards and forwards with your hand on the head tube, feeling for any play at the headset.

10 Align the handlebars and fully tighten the stem pinch bolts. Take the bike for a short test ride and then check the headset and bolts again.

Cartridge bearings

1 Sometimes sealed cartridge bearings can be given an extra lease of life. Spin the bearing in your hand, and if it feels rough or gritty carefully use a sharp knife blade to ease out the seal.

2 Remove the seal and flush the old grease out with a suitable solvent, then repack the bearing with fresh grease. Carefully refit the seal to the bearing.

Replacing and adjusting threaded headset bearings

1 It may be necessary to disconnect the brakes on some bikes, but normally it's possible to release the quill stem and remove the bars and quill as a complete unit. Secure the bars to the top tube with a tie wrap.

2 Unscrew and then remove the top lockring. It's possible to remove the upper nut with a pair of adjustable spanners. However, you'll need the correct spanner for the lower nut.

3 Many bikes will have a washer fitted below the top nut. Remove this, using a small screwdriver to prise it free if necessary.

4 Use a tie wrap to secure the forks to the down tube, or have an assistant hold the forks in place. With the forks secure remove the lower nut.

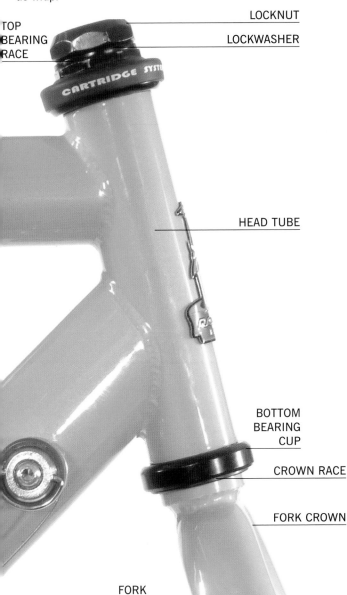

TOP
BEARING
RACE —————— LOCKNUT

—————— LOCKWASHER

HEAD TUBE ——————

BOTTOM
BEARING
CUP ——————

CROWN RACE ——————

FORK CROWN ——————

FORK ——————

5 Slowly remove the forks and recover the bearings. Most forks will have caged or cartridge bearings, but some will have loose bearings fitted.

6 With the forks removed, thoroughly inspect the head tube and the condition of the crown race. Clean or replace the bearings and refit the forks.

7 Refit the upper bearing cap, washer and lock nut. Now adjust the threaded bearing top cover so that no play is present. Hold the lower nut in position with one spanner and tighten the lock nut with another. It may take a few attempts to get this just right.

Suspension forks: strip down and overhaul

Whilst not an entirely new concept, suspension forks have only come to the fore in recent years. Early models usually featured various combinations of a structural foam material commonly referred to as an elastomer. These elastomers were both the suspension and the damping. Unfortunately, the constant compression of the material eventually led to its breakdown. Low-cost suspension forks may well still feature an elastomer of some description, but more often than not even cheap forks now have springs fitted.

Middle- and top-of-the-range forks feature numerous adjustments to control the speed at which the fork compresses (compression adjustment) and rebounds (the rate at which the fork returns to its resting position). Compression and rebound rates are adjusted by controlling the flow of oil through the fork internals. On many top-of-the-range forks, it's possible to stop the flow of oil completely and effectively lock the fork. This lockout feature transforms it into a virtually rigid fork, ideally suited for climbing.

Coil-sprung forks are common on many entry-level forks. However, air-sprung forks provide an extremely lightweight solution at the middle to top end of the market. All suspension forks require maintenance, though the amount required varies with each manufacturer. You should at the very least clean and wash down the fork stanchions after every ride. As a general rule of thumb the lowers should be removed, cleaned and lubricated every six months or so. Of course, this all depends on the type of fork fitted and more importantly where the bike has been ridden. A short-travel fork fitted to a commuter bike may only require a service once a year. A long-travel fork fitted to a serious off-road mountain bike may require a service of the lowers (at the very least) every other month. The fork manufacturer will provide general service intervals, but they should only be used as a guide.

FORK OIL

The viscosity of an oil is determined by its 'weight'. This is an SAE (Society of Automotive Engineers) international standard, so that in theory a '10' weight oil should be the same regardless of manufacturer. However, this isn't always the case, so it's often best practice to stick to the fork manufacturer's recommended fluid. Oil for bicycle suspension forks ranges in weight from approximately .25wt to 7.5wt.

WHEN YOU NEED TO DO THIS:
■ According to the manufacturer's service schedule.
■ If the fork action become sticky or the fork damping deteriorates.

TIME:
■ Allow at least an hour the first time you service your forks.

DIFFICULTY: ✓✓✓✓✓
■ This can appear a very daunting job at first. After you've serviced your forks a few times it becomes considerably easier.

AIR SUSPENSION FORKS
Though air suspension forks are becoming more common than spring forks, they're far more complex to strip down and overhaul. That's why if you have issues with your air forks, the best port of call is your trusted local bike shop. If you're looking to set the air pressure dependent on rider weight, use an air shock pump as used on page 171. Your forks should feature ideal psi based on rider weight.

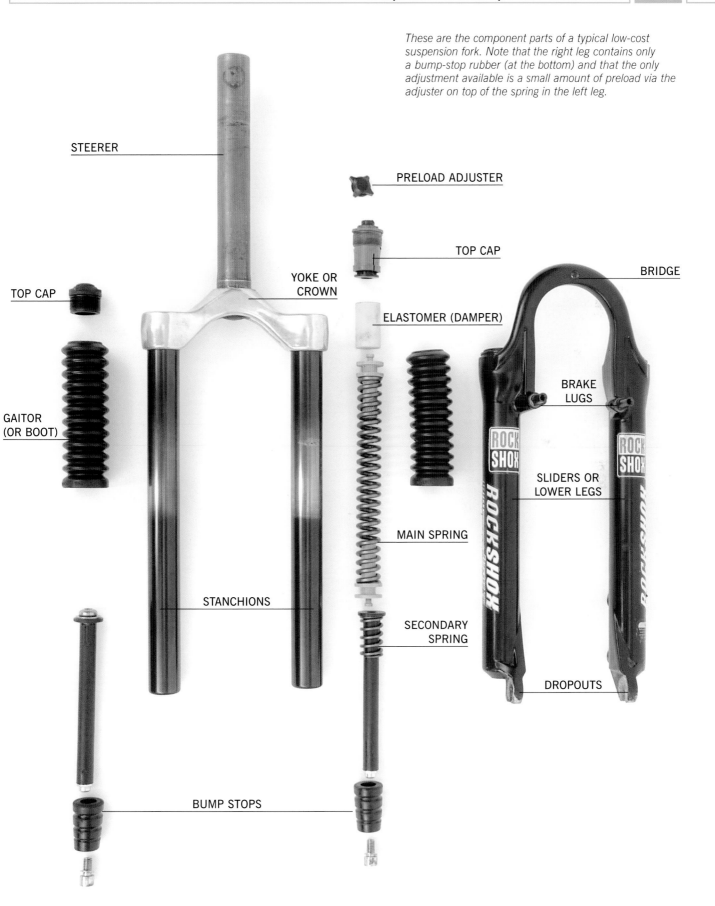

These are the component parts of a typical low-cost suspension fork. Note that the right leg contains only a bump-stop rubber (at the bottom) and that the only adjustment available is a small amount of preload via the adjuster on top of the spring in the left leg.

STEERER

PRELOAD ADJUSTER

TOP CAP

YOKE OR CROWN

BRIDGE

TOP CAP

ELASTOMER (DAMPER)

GAITOR (OR BOOT)

BRAKE LUGS

SLIDERS OR LOWER LEGS

MAIN SPRING

STANCHIONS

SECONDARY SPRING

DROPOUTS

BUMP STOPS

Stripping and cleaning of a typical fork

1 Remove the forks from the bike and mount them in a workstand. You could also improvise and use a collapsible workbench (as pictured), protecting the legs with a rag. Slacken the lower bolts, but don't remove them.

2 Using a soft-faced mallet, drive down the locking bolts to free the stanchions. With the stanchions freed remove the bolts completely.

3 Carefully remove the lower fork assembly from the stanchions and place them to one side.

4 Place the stanchions in a suitable vice and remove the adjuster for the preload and both top caps.

5 Remove the fork gaiters and recover the bump stops. Turn the forks over and remove the spring and elastomer. Note that on this fork the right leg doesn't contain a spring.

6 Remove the dust and oil seal from the fork lowers and then thoroughly clean out the lowers with a suitable solvent.

7 The ideal is to use a nylon seal driver to fit the new combined oil and dust seal. However, if approached carefully, you could use a suitable socket.

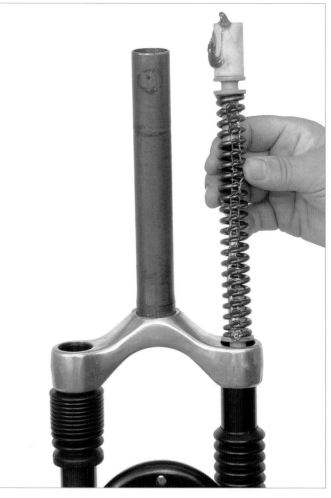

8 Clean and inspect the stanchions. Lubricate the spring and elastomer assembly with a suitable suspension grease.

Fitting new seals and lower leg service

1 With the forks removed from the bicycle, protect the forks and clamp them firmly in a workbench. Remove the lower nuts with a suitable socket or spanner.

2 Using a block of wood to protect the threads from damage, drive the inners free from the lower legs.

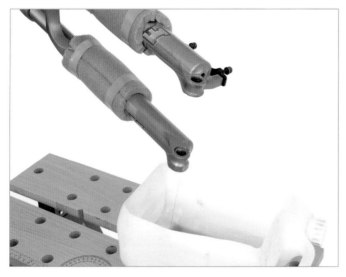

3 Invert the forks and drain the oil from them into a suitable container.

4 Carefully remove the stanchions and then, using a suitable spanner or screwdriver, gently prise free the oil seals. These forks also have a foam seal below the combined oil and wiper seal. Remove this.

5 Clean and inspect the stanchions and lower legs. We used a suitable solvent and a lint-free rag wrapped around an old bicycle spoke to clean the lowers.

6 Soak the new foam seals in oil and refit them with, ideally, a nylon seal driver or a suitable socket (pictured).

7 Lightly lubricate the stanchions and carefully slide them back into the fork lower legs, taking care not to damage the new seals.

8 Invert the forks and add the correct amount of oil to each leg. Push the fork lowers fully home, fit the new crush washers and nuts, and tighten to the recommended torque.

Suspension bike frames

Full suspension mountain bike frames rely upon bearings or bushes to allow the rear swinging arm to move. Early designs were commonly known as URT (unified rear triangle) designs, where the drivetrain was part of the rear suspension. This design is still to be found on some very low-cost full-suspension bikes, but most full-suspension designs today feature an independent rear triangle (IRT) suspension system. On IRT designs the bottom bracket is always part of the main bicycle frame.

IRT suspension systems may be a simple single-pivot design or a complicated multiple linkage and multi-pivot design. On single-pivot bikes the axle path of the rear wheel is a constant arc, regardless of the compression of the suspension. On multi-pivot designs the axle path of the rear wheel isn't constant, as the rear wheel isn't rotating around a fixed point. However, some designs that appear to be multi-pivot are in fact simple single-pivot designs that use a linkage system to compress the rear shock absorber.

All full-suspension bikes must have a spring and some method of damping the oscillations of the spring. These functions are combined in a single spring and damper unit. Note, however, that very cheap full-suspension bikes may have a coil spring fitted but no damping system.

The spring may be a coil spring or an air spring. Coil springs are available in several spring strengths to suit the weight of the rider. Air springs are adjustable to suit the rider by varying the air pressure in the spring. Depending on the quality of the rear shock absorber and spring unit various tuning functions will be available. These may include controls for adjusting the compression damping and the rebound damping. Some also feature a lockout function that effectively transforms the rear suspension into a fully rigid bike for climbing on- or off-road.

Because there are so many moving parts on a full-suspension bike attention should always be paid to any play or excess movement in the pivot points. Most bikes use cartridge bearings for the various linkages and pivots, and these are often prone to wear. Any unusual clunks, knocks or rattles from the rear suspension should be investigated immediately.

Most suspension bikes use cartridge bearings. Each manufacturer specifies their own size and diameter, although most of these will be standard, easily available bearings. The worn bearings can normally be driven from the frame or link arm with a suitable socket or punch. The hardest bearings to remove are those that sit in an almost blind housing. If the inner race collapses and leaves the outer race trapped in the frame or link arm, it's impossible to get to the rear to remove it. In this case the only option available is to hire or borrow a blind bearing puller. This tool uses a slide hammer and expanding wedge to lock on to the remains of the outer race.

Replacing rear shock bushes

1 A simple bush removal and installation tool will be required to service the glacier-type bushing fitted to many rear shock absorbers.

WHEN YOU NEED TO DO THIS:
■ When play develops in the bearings or shock absorber bushes.

TIME:
■ Allow up to two hours or more if you're replacing all the bearings in a complex suspension frame.

DIFFICULTY:
/ / / / / /
■ Replacing bearings can be one of the most difficult jobs to undertake on any bicycle.

2 Assemble the extractor and pull the old bush out of the shock and into the main body of the extractor tool. Clean the eye of the shock and inspect it for damage.

3 Reverse the tool and use it to draw the new bush into the eye of the shock.

Replacing bearings in a suspension frame

1 Most bearings are a press-fit in either the bicycle frame or the rocker plates. Remove the rocker plate with a suitable hex key.

2 We used a suitable piece of wood with various diameter holes drilled in it as a jig. We then used an old socket to drive the bearing out of the arm and through the appropriate hole in the jig.

3 To fit the new bearings we used a combination of old sockets, washers and a length of threaded bar. Always ensure that the sockets only bear on the outer race of the bearing.

Setting up a suspension bike

All full-suspension bikes require the correct set-up to maximise the potential of the suspension. The first thing to do is to set the initial travel. This is often referred to as setting the 'sag'. The starting point for setting the sag is around 25% of the total available travel of the bike. However, there's no hard-and-fast rule for this setting. For example, on a short-travel bike you may only want to set the sag at around 10% of the available travel. Conversely, on a long-travel downhill bike you may wish to set the initial sag at around 30% of the total available. Some experimentation will always be required to find a happy medium.

The terrain that the bike will be ridden over is another consideration. A short-travel suspension bike that may only be ridden along a canal towpath could easily be set up with the initial sag set at 30%, as it's unlikely that any terrain will be encountered that will use up the total available travel.

With the initial sag set correctly, attention should then be paid to the various damping controls. These will vary depending on the quality of the bike, but most will have some form of rebound and compression damping control. A good starting point is to set all the available adjustments to the midpoint. If, for example, the rebound control has ten stages of adjustment then the initial setting should be at five. As ever this can only be a guide – the best solution will always be to ride the bike and make adjustments as you go. Some riders prefer a lively feel to the suspension and will run their damping controls at the minimum settings; others will prefer a more solid feel and will opt to run any damping controls at or near their maximum.

If you're setting up the front suspension on a hard-tail, *ie* a bike with no rear suspension, then the same procedure should be followed as when setting up a full-suspension bike. With the sag correctly set and the damping controls adjusted it's time to take the bike for an extended test ride. After a long test ride it's worth checking how much travel has been used. Ideally the suspension should have bottomed out and moved through all the available travel at least once or twice during the ride. Check that full travel has been achieved after you've passed a particular rocky section of the ride. If your test ride is urban then riding off kerbs and up steps is a good way to see full travel has been achieved or if the suspension needs further adjustment.

WHEN YOU NEED TO DO THIS:
- Before the first ride if it's a new bike.
- Whenever you've upgraded or changed suspension components.

TIME:
- Allow 20 minutes to set up the suspension. If you include a test ride and minor adjustments then allow an hour at the very least.

DIFFICULTY: ✗✗✗
- The basic setting is fairly straightforward – getting the suspension perfect to suit your riding style or the terrain can take a while.

COIL SPRINGS
Coil springs for rear shocks are available in a large range of weights. This weight isn't the weight of the spring but the amount of weight needed to compress it a certain amount. On mountain bikes this is normally expressed as a pounds per inch figure. The maximum shock stroke a spring is suitable for will also be listed. You also need to know the length of your existing spring. Springs are available from 350lb through to 800lb.

1 Regardless of manufacturers' claims the available travel on a full-suspension bike is always determined by the stroke of the rear shock. However, this isn't the total travel available at the rear wheel.

2 Many shocks and forks have an O-ring fitted as standard. If not, then temporarily fit a tie wrap. Gently mount the bike and then dismount. Now check how far down the shock the O-ring has moved. Alter the air pressure or increase the preload on the spring if necessary so that approximately 10% to 30% of the available travel has been used. This is the sag setting.

3 Most rear coil shocks will have a bump-stop fitted. Use a thin screwdriver to lift this from its seat. This will now act as a travel indicator. Preload can be adjusted on a coil shock by rotating the collar on top of the spring. However, if you need to screw down the coil more than two or three full revolutions to set the suspension correctly you may want to consider changing to a higher spring-rate coil.

4 Use a shock pump to add or remove air from the high-pressure chamber of an air shock. Some high-end rear shocks will also have a separate air chamber that may also require adjustment if you find you're travelling through the available travel too easily.

5 With the sag set correctly, next adjust the damping controls. For most forks and rear shocks the starting point is normally midway through the available range. If you're unsure where this is exactly, then fully wind in and then fully wind out the control dial, counting the number of turns required to move from full on to full off. Select the midpoint as a starting point.

6 The same procedure can then be used to set up the front suspension. If you have a coil front suspension fork you may only have a limited choice of replacement springs, so if you're particularly heavy or light consider changing to an air front suspension fork. When you have arrived at your preferred settings, write them down and store in a safe place.

CHAPTER

SAFETY, SECURITY AND ACCESSORIES

Helmets

A good helmet that fits properly should be worn at all times while riding. With the vast range of styles and designs available there's really no excuse for not wearing one, so take your time and try on as many different types from as many different manufacturers as possible. A good-looking helmet that fits well is more likely to get worn than a poor-fitting and unfashionable one. Having said that, fit is always more important than looks.

The first generation of modern bicycle helmets were manufactured from polystyrene and had a simple stretch cover. Most modern helmets are still fabricated from polystyrene but now have a thin plastic outer shell taped or bonded to the polystyrene. BMX helmets tend to be made from a rigid plastic with a thinner polystyrene inner core. Full-faced helmets for downhill riding are again made either from a rigid plastic outer shell, or indeed a carbon fibre outer shell, and then have an inner polystyrene liner.

All helmets, regardless of their composition, must conform to certain safety standards. Those most commonly referred to are EN 1078 and Snell B95. All bicycle helmets sold in Great Britain and Europe must conform to the European EN 1078 standard. Older helmets may conform to the superseded UK standard of BS 6863. However, given that the majority of these helmets will now be well over ten years old they should be replaced anyway, as most manufacturers and some of the various international standards recommend the replacement of a helmet after a maximum of five years regardless of use, as the polystyrene and various other components tend to degrade with age. Note, however, that Bell, Met and Giro all recommend helmet replacement after three years. To many consumers this may seem slightly excessive, especially for the occasional rider who only wears their helmet during the summer months.

1 All helmets should be provided with varying thicknesses of foam pads to customise the fit. These pads are designed to fine-tune the fit of the helmet, not to compensate for a poorly fitting one.

2 Most helmets now feature a retention strap that's adjustable at the rear. This strap can be adjusted for a snug fit, and because of its positioning it helps to stop the helmet tipping forwards or backwards.

3 Always position the helmet correctly on your head. This helmet is tipped backwards, exposing the forehead. The helmet is the right size – it's just incorrectly fitted.

4 With the helmet correctly positioned the forehead will be covered. Adjust the straps so the adjustable buckles fit snugly below the ears and the chinstrap is secure.

Bike security

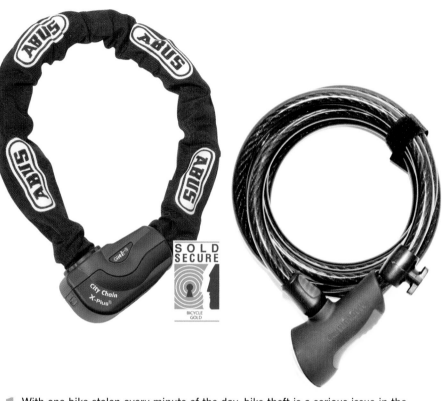

1 With one bike stolen every minute of the day, bike theft is a serious issue in the UK. A simple cable lock will deter the opportunistic thief, but high-quality U-bolt locks will always be the preferred choice. In vulnerable areas consider using more than one lock.

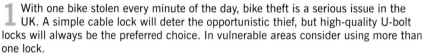

2 Always lock your bike to an immovable object, preferably an official bike stand. If you have quick-release wheels fitted then remove the front wheel and lock it behind the bike. If you have a quick release fitted to the seat post then consider removing the saddle and taking it with you.

3 The golden rule when locking up your bike is to always make the locking mechanism as inaccessible as possible. If you find it hard to access the locking mechanism then a potential thief will have the same problem.

Safety clothing

1 Most cycle-specific clothing will incorporate multiple reflective surfaces. This jacket has reflective patches and the provision for a rear light to be fitted.

2 Many cyclists consider gloves an essential item of clothing. A wide variety of styles are available, from traditional track mitts through to full-finger waterproof winter gloves.

3 For casual use a reflective belt and armbands are easy to carry around and are very effective.

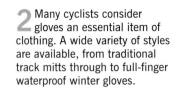

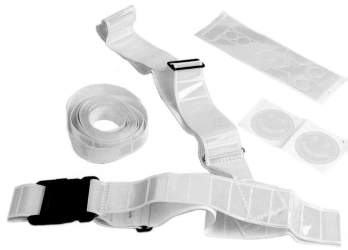

Bike lights

1 Long gone are the days of traditional bike lights with the cumbersome fittings and leaking batteries. These rear lights all feature LED (light emitting diode) technology. Most have several modes of operation, from a solid constant beam to a multitude of flashing combinations.

2 Reflectors should always be fitted to any bike, with spoke reflectors being particularly effective when viewed from the side. In the UK a rear reflector and pedal reflectors are a mandatory legal requirement.

3 Front lights are also important. LED technology has enabled manufacturers to produce a very bright light with very low power consumption. Brackets are also available to allow a pencil-type torch to be used as a front light.

LEGAL REQUIREMENTS

Any new bike sold in the UK must conform to the 'Pedal Bicycles Safety Regulations' (PBSR), which requires that every new bike sold must have:

- A red reflector at the rear.
- A white reflector at the front.
- Yellow reflectors on the front and rear of each pedal.
- White or yellow reflectors on both wheels.
- A bell.
- Front and rear brakes, with the front brake mounted on the right-hand side.

It should be noted that these regulations only apply at the point of sale. As soon as the bicycle has been removed from the shop you're free (whilst not recommended) to remove any or all of these safety features. However, if you ride your bike at night it *must* be fitted with front and rear bicycle lights. Since the appropriate road traffic lighting regulations were amended in 2005 it has become perfectly legal to use a flashing light on a bicycle. This must flash between 60 and 240 times per minute. If a flashing light is fitted no other additional lighting is required. A rear reflector and pedal reflectors must also be fitted for night-time use.

Regardless of all the legal requirements, and because cyclists are a vulnerable group of road users, with over 200 cyclists killed or seriously injured every month on Britain's roads, there's absolutely no reason why all cyclists shouldn't be visible to all other road users at all times.

4 For serious off-road use and night-time commuting away from urban areas a wide range of high-power, rechargeable front lights is now available. These incorporate the latest advances in LED technology. This is a helmet-mounted light with an output of over 1,000 lumens.

Apparel & accessories

Beyond the important issues of safety and security, there's a whole load of kit out there to enhance your cycling experience, whether you're looking to commute efficiently as possible or are looking to train smart for your first sportive (mass bike event).

When it comes to clothing, you'll find that three of the key terms regularly used are: wicking, breathability and insulation. Wicking refers to transferring perspiration from your body to the outside environment so you don't overheat. The right material helps this process – as it does with breathability. Again, though it might be cold outside, once you begin cycling you soon generate huge amounts of heat. Good clothing will ensure air still circulates between you and your clothing so you don't 'boil in the bag'. As for insulation, some days you really will need layers to fend off the sub-zero temperatures.

As well as clothing, we list other items to enhance your riding, as well as featuring tools for the cyclist who's looking to gauge how hard they're working. These range from the simple bike computer to more expensive power meters.

◀ HEART RATE MONITORS
Unlike their more-expensive sibling – the power meter – a heart rate monitor is an affordable tool to guide your training. Simply find your maximum heart rate (max HR) by riding flat out for 20mins and noting the peak figure. You can then ride by training zones depending on your physiological goals. For example, around 70% of your maximum improves your ability to burn fat, while 90% increases speed.

▲ SUNGLASSES Cycling eyewear isn't just for summer – all-year-round glasses keep out bugs, wind and even snow. What changes is the lens tint with many models on the market featuring interchangeable lenses. That means a standard shaded lens when the sun shines; a lens with a yellow tinge will brighten up the most overcast day; while a clear lens is ideal when riding after dark.

◀ PANNIERS Pannier racks and bags are ideal for touring cyclists and commuters, helping you to cart around your gear, whether it's commuting essentials like laptops and folders, to longer rides that might demand overnight stops. Cue a pannier bag comprising clothing, toothbrush and even a tent! Whether you can fit a pannier rack remains to be seen as your bike needs the relevant bosses for pannier attachment. These will be at the front and rear of your bike.

▲ NECK WEAR These versatile garments, colloquially called Snood after the famous neckwear manufacturer, are primarily used by cyclists to protect their necks from winter draughts, though you can also use them as a scarf, balaclava, headband or even a wristband. Like base layers, these are often made from polyester to add breathability while transferring sweat.

◀ GILETS These simple, sleeveless tops are popular in road riding as they keep your torso warm without overheating. There are two types of gilet: a lightweight, packable gilet for spring and autumn riding; and heavier, insulating alternatives for colder conditions. The lightweight versions are more common as, though they don't provide much in terms of insulation, they do fend off wind. Heavier gilets are less common as many riders just pitch for windproof jackets instead.

▶ BIKE JACKETS Your upper body's susceptible to greater cooling than your lower body because, unlike your legs, it remains relatively static. Enter the appliance of science. Top-end windproof bike jackets utilise cutting-edge materials to deflect the wind but without creating an uncomfortable boil-in-the-bag effect. Windstopper is a respected material patented by Gore. Essentially it's a membrane that sits between the inner lining and outer fabric to protect you from the wind but not to the detriment of breathability.

▶ CHAMOIS CREAM Chamois cream is an anti-bacterial, viscous substance that resembles moisturiser. However, instead of smoothing out wrinkles, it's designed to be slathered on your bottom/perineum with the aim of reducing friction between skin and clothing. This prevents chafing, which can lead to saddle sores or, even worse, an abscess.

▲ BASE LAYERS Technical pieces of clothing that provide the dual roles of insulation and breathability. Manmade fabrics like polyester are common because the structure of the fibres wicks sweat away from the body and to the environment quicker than cotton, so doesn't become saturated as quickly. Mind you, Merino wool's also used for its natural performance properties. A good-fitting base layer should be figure-hugging but not too tight, as this reduces its warming effect. Conversely, too loose and you'll fail to wick sweat from the body.

▲ ENERGY GELS Where once the pros were fuelled on baguettes and wine, now they use energy gels. These handy sachets easily fit into your rear pocket, though you can always squeeze extra gels into a Bento box or saddle bag. One of the most convenient sachets is arguably the SiS Go gel, which is described as isotonic, meaning a water chaser isn't required. (Many gels can be a tad cloying, particularly when they're highly viscous.) You can also complement your fuelling with energy drinks and bars.

▲ BIB LONGS These may offend your work colleagues but they're vital for road riding during winter months. They're commonly constructed from Lycra, which not only adds warmth but also offers freedom of movement – vital when pedalling. Importantly, bib longs come with a padded chamois to aid comfort in the saddle. Some come with loops around the bottom of the legs to keep things in place. Shorter versions are available for warmer rides.

◀ POWER METERS Scan the professional peloton and the greatest impact on how the likes of Sagan, Cavendish and Froome train is the power meter. As the name suggests, power meters measure the amount of wattage you generate on a bike. How they do this relies on myriads of electronics and accurate algorithms. There are various models on the market, ranging from Garmin's Vector that determines data from the pedals to Stages' crank-based power meters – currently used by Team Sky – to the Powertap G3, which measures power at the hub of the rear wheel. This data is wirelessly transmitted to a head unit on your handlebars. One for the committed roadie.

▲ AEROBARS Aerobars steer you further forward onto your cockpit for a lower and drag-reducing frontal profile. They're not for riding in groups – but popular at midweek time trials – meaning you want to be flexible. That's why a set of clip-on aerobars is perfect for all levels of roadie.

▶ URBAN CLOTHING Cycling apparel isn't all about Lycra and padded gussets – there's an increasingly stylish sector of clothing that appeals to the more casual rider, though still comes with cycle-specific features. Brands like Rapha and Café du Cycliste have aesthetically pleasing ranges of jackets, trousers and shirts, complete with useful additions like rear pockets to store keys, extra-strong chinos for durability and subtle reflectives on the trouser legs.

◀ BIKE COMPUTERS The humble bike computer's not so humble these days, with models from Polar and Suunto providing enough data and information to satiate the most committed technophile's appetite. We're talking GPS capability, power data and metres climbed. There are still more rudimentary but still-useful computers around, which measure distance ridden and calories burnt.

▶ TURBO TRAINER This is a device that clamps around the quick-release skewer on your rear wheel, usually suspended in an A-frame. Your rear wheel rests against a roller with resistance provided by a unit connected to said roller. This is the primary source of a trainer's difference as that resistance can derive from either magnetic or fluid means. Both do a job, though the slightly more-expensive fluid version is quieter. There's also the increasingly popular direct-drive category that clamps to your dropouts.

Bike racks

Head into a large bike retailer and you'll be confronted with a plethora of racks to carry your bike safely from A to B. It can feel akin to entering a maze but each has been designed to suit specific situations. How far and how frequently will you look to carry bikes? Will you be taking a number of bikes or just the one? Do you prefer bikes stored on the roof or off the back? Yes, questions are many but the first one, which can be answered swiftly, is how much are you willing to spend? If your bike of choice is slick carbon and costs the price of a new car, you probably won't want to risk transporting your bike on a rack that costs the same as one of your tyres. Once you've worked out a price, you then need to decide on which of the three main racks you go for: roof-mounted, towbar-mounted or boot-mounted…

◄ BOOT-MOUNTED RACK The final popular option is attaching a rack to your boot. These tend to be the least expensive option, which means they're often the least secure. That's because the main structures holding them to your vehicle are a collection of straps that hook around the lip of your vehicle's boot. Rubber or foam 'feet' grip your vehicle with the entire unit pulled taut via those straps. Bikes are attached on an arm extending from the unit with bikes clamped via the top tube. They're versatile but they must be fitted properly; if not, they're liable to be a danger. Cheaper hooks could also damage paintwork, so go for a higher-end model.

▼ TOWBAR-MOUNTED RACK Towbar-mounted racks, or hitch-mounted racks in the US, connect to the towbar at the rear of your vehicle. They're often more expensive than the other two styles, but that's potentially a price worth paying for ease of loading and unloading bikes. You also won't have to attach them to your roof, which puts many cyclists off.

Towbar-mounted racks usually hold bikes by their wheels with an arm securing the front wheel. Alternatively, they'll clamp the bikes into place by their top tubes. Either way, they can accommodate up to five bikes. Rather neatly, most feature hinged loading sections, which means you have access to your boot without having to remove your flotilla of bikes.

The only real downside is the price, not only of the rack but you'll require a towbar fitted unless, of course, you already have one. Australian riders also require an accessory number plate to add to the rack if it conceals your current rear number.

▲ ROOF-MOUNTED RACK The majority of roof racks comprise 'feet' that attach to your roof and cross bars that the accessories attach to, but this is a job that's ideally ticked off by a professional as it can be quite fiddly and, of course, you don't want to compromise with safety.

Bike racks for your vehicle's roof come in two forms: where you must remove the front wheel or racks that allow both wheels to remain on the bike. You'll find that front-wheel removal keeps the bike lower (which is good for tall vehicles) and are very stable. On the downside, it means you'll have to store your front wheel in your boot. Bike racks that keep the wheels on aren't quite as stable but they're easier to attach and remove. In general, a locking system will keep the bikes safe when parked. Roof racks are also handy if you want to transport other bulky items like ladders or sports gear like kayaks. There are also roof racks that use suction cups. Whichever roof rack you use, just remember they're on your roof – this is especially important in overflow car parks that feature frame restrictions! They also add extra drag, which equates to extra petrol.

CHAPTER

APPENDICES

Troubleshooting

General

Riding discomfort
☐ Adjust bar reach/position
☐ Adjust saddle fore/aft position

Riding feels bumpy
☐ Tyres under-inflated
☐ Fit larger volume tyres

Saddle discomfort
☐ Adjust saddle position/angle
☐ Try padded cycling shorts
☐ Fit better-quality saddle

Handlebar discomfort
☐ Adjust handlebar angle
☐ Try different grips/padded bar tape
☐ Try cycling mitts or gloves
☐ Try a different bar shape

Foot discomfort
☐ Try shoes with firmer sole
☐ Convert to clipless pedals
☐ Check foot position

Bike tiring to ride
☐ Tyres under-inflated
☐ Saddle too low
☐ Brakes rubbing wheel
☐ Tyre rubbing frame or mudguard
☐ Transmission, chain corroded
☐ Inappropriate use of gears
☐ Fit narrower/slicker tyres

Bike unstable, especially at speed
☐ Tyres under-inflated
☐ Wheel/headset bearings loose
☐ Bent forks or frame
☐ Wheels need truing

Bike rattles
☐ Mudguards, rack or other accessories loose
☐ Luggage too heavy, high or far back
☐ Rack insufficiently rigid

Scraping sounds
☐ Mudguards rubbing on tyre
☐ Mud flap or debris caught inside mudguard
☐ Chain rubbing chain guard

Small bolts work loose
☐ Refit with Loctite thread compound

Gears

REAR DERAILLEUR

Indexing imprecise/slow
☐ Cable tension needs adjustment
☐ Cable needs greasing/replacing
☐ Derailleur or its hanger bent/misaligned
☐ Incompatible components
☐ Incorrect cable/cable housing/end-caps

Can't get biggest cog
☐ Derailleur's 'low' screw needs adjustment
☐ Cable tension needs adjustment

Chain/derailleur goes into wheel
☐ Derailleur's 'low' screw needs adjustment
☐ Derailleur or its hanger bent
☐ Check spokes and wheel OK

Can't get smallest cog
☐ Derailleur's 'high' screw needs adjustment
☐ Cable tension needs adjustment

Chain leaves smallest rear cog
☐ Derailleur's 'high' screw needs adjustment

FRONT DERAILLEUR

Chain jams during shift
☐ Derailleur too low
☐ Chain too short

Chain leaves/won't get small ring
☐ Derailleur's 'low' screw needs adjustment

Chain leaves/won't get big ring
☐ Derailleur's 'high' screw needs adjustment

Chain won't shift/slow to shift
☐ Derailleur too high
☐ Derailleur's mounting angle incorrect
☐ Cage plates need slight bending inwards

FRONT AND REAR DERAILLEUR

Gears self-change/go out of adjustment
☐ Lever's friction screw needs tightening
☐ Somebody oiled a friction lever!
☐ Cable clamp bolt loose
☐ Cable end-caps missing

Shifting requires a lot of effort
☐ Cable routing incorrect
☐ Cable needs lubrication/replacement

HUB GEARS

Hub gear slips (all models)
☐ Cable tension needs adjustment
☐ Cable clamps/guides loose
☐ Wheel slipping – nuts loose?
☐ Hub's internal parts worn
☐ Chain/sprocket severely worn

Chain, pedals and cranks

Chain broken
☐ Chain joined incorrectly
☐ Chain worn

Chain jumps under load
☐ Chain and/or cassette cogs worn
☐ Stiff link

Chain noisy
☐ Chain needs lubrication
☐ Chain worn

Regular clicking or jumping
☐ Chain has stiff link
☐ Crank cotter pin loose/worn
☐ Crank bolt loose
☐ Bent cog/chainwheel tooth
☐ Worn chain

Irregular clicking/creaking when pedalling
☐ Pedal cage or bearings disintegrating
☐ Bottom bracket bearings need attention
☐ Loose spokes
☐ Chainwheel bolts need greasing
☐ Crank loose on axle
☐ Last resort – grease axle taper

Pedalling feels strange
☐ Cranks or pedals bent or loose

Back-pedalling feels stiff
☐ Hub gear or single-speed chain too tight
☐ Hub gear bearings too tight

Irregular knocking sound
☐ Bottom bracket bearings need attention

FREEWHEELS

Freewheel 'knocks' while pedalling
☐ Its bearings are working loose!

Freewheel spins noisily
☐ Its bearings are worn/need cleaning/need lubrication

Freewheel slips/binds
☐ Mechanism needs attention/replacement

FREEHUBS

Freehub slips/binds
☐ Shimano – replace freehub body
☐ Most others – overhaul it

Cassette 'knocks' in riding
☐ Cassette lockring loose

Brakes

Insufficient brake power/cable pull
☐ Cable needs adjusting
☐ Quick release needs resetting
☐ Brake blocks worn
☐ Oil on rim
☐ Cable corroded or needs lubrication
☐ Brake lever mounting clamp loose
☐ Incompatible brake/lever combination

Brakes quickly lose power
☐ Cable clamp bolt insufficiently tight
☐ Brake blocks not tight
☐ Cable housing missing end-caps

Brakes don't release properly
☐ Pivot bolt(s) too tight
☐ Cable corroded or needs lubrication
☐ Brake block position incorrect
☐ Spring tension of brake incorrect

Brakes noisy/squeal
☐ Brake blocks old and hard – replace
☐ Brake blocks need toeing-in
☐ Rim needs cleaning

Brakes judder/grab
☐ Brake blocks need 'Toeing-in'
☐ Wheel rim bent or dented
☐ Brake pivots too loose
☐ Headset bearings loose

Brakes stiff to apply
☐ Cable corroded or not lubricated
☐ Cable routing too short or too long
☐ Spring tension of cantilever brakes set incorrectly

Brake levers creak in use
☐ Spray mounting and pivots with thin lubricant

Poor braking in rain
☐ Fit better brake blocks/alloy rims

Wheels and tyres

Tyre deflates slowly
☐ Slow puncture
☐ Valve loose or leaking

Tyre deflates quickly
☐ Puncture or blow-out!

Repetitive punctures
☐ Puncture cause still in tyre
☐ Rim tape missing
☐ Protruding spoke
☐ Tyre worn
☐ Tyres under-inflated
☐ Tyre levers used to fit tyre

Tyre unevenly mounted
☐ Refit correctly

Wheel out of true
☐ Broken spoke
☐ Spokes need adjustment

Clicking noises from hub
☐ Bearings need attention
☐ Wheels have side-to-side play
☐ Wheel bearings loose
☐ Wheel nuts loose
☐ Broken wheel spindle

Bars and saddle

Bars don't appear or feel right
☐ Check alignment
☐ Check for bent bars

Bars creak
☐ Bar/stem interface needs greasing
☐ Stem/fork interface needs greasing
☐ Bars are developing a crack!

Bars rotate in stem
☐ Stem bolt insufficiently tight
☐ Incorrect matching of bars and stem

Handlebar stem moves in fork
☐ Handlebar expander bolt insufficiently tight

Handlebar stem seized in fork
☐ Stem wasn't greased – try soaking with spray lubricant

Saddle tilts or moves
☐ Post's cradle bolt insufficiently tight
☐ Saddle clamp bolt insufficiently tight
☐ Saddle clamp too high on post

Saddle noisy or creaking
☐ Spray clamp, springs etc with light lubricant

Seat post seized in frame
☐ Post wasn't greased – try soaking with spray lubricant
☐ Post diameter too large

Seat post moves in frame
☐ Seat lug clamp bolt insufficiently tight
☐ Post diameter too small

Frame and forks

Forks judder
☐ Headset bearings loose
☐ Brakes grabbing rim

Bike tends to pull to one side
☐ Wheel (especially front) not centralised
☐ Forks or frame bent

Steering/handling strange
☐ Tyres under-inflated
☐ Headset too tight/too loose
☐ Headset worn
☐ Forks/frame bent

Headset continually works loose
☐ Locknut insufficiently tight
☐ Worn headset
☐ Forks/frame bent
☐ Too many ball bearings!

Common tyre sizes

Replacing tyres can feel like negotiating a minefield, especially as measurements across mountain biking and road riding mix imperial and metric. Take 700c tyres, which are common on most road bikes. Recent years have seen an explosion in these in mountain biking, albeit they're referred to as 29-inch.

There's further confusion with tyre width (below we focus on tyre diameter), whose label follows the tyre's diameter. For road, this could be 700 x 23 (mm) up to 700 x 28. As a general rule, you'll normally be okay with a tyre either one size up or one size down from the one that you're using. So if you're using a 700 x 28 tyre, you could upsize to 700 x 32 for a slightly softer ride or downsize to 700 x 25 for a firmer effort.

Imperial	Metric	Application
29	622	700c standard road; modern mountain bikes; hybrid bikes
27.5	584	650b mountain bikes; some road bikes
27	630	Old road bikes
26	559	Mountain bikes
24	507	Small mountain bikes
20	406	BMX and children's bikes
16	349	Children's bikes and folding bikes
12	203	Children's bikes and folding bikes

Tightening torques

Please note that the figures given to your right are only a general guide. If you're in any doubt, consult the manufacturer for their specific tightening torque figures. Also note that the majority of bolts and components used on bikes have maximum torques printed on them.

Component		Torque (Nm)
M5 bolt		4–6
M6 bolt		7–10
M8 bolt		16–24
M10 bolt		35–50
Bolt-in wheel nuts		20–30
Bottom bracket	Shimano Hollowtech II	34.5–49.1
	Campagnolo Ultra-Torque	35
	FSA	39.2–49
	Race Face	47.5
	Truvativ	33.9–40.1
	White Industries	27

Component		Torque (Nm)
Brake lever mounting bolts		4–8
Cable pinch bolts		3–4
Cartridge bottom brackets		35–50
Cassette lock ring		30–50
Chainring bolts		5–7
Crank arm bolts (spline and square taper)		25–50
Disc rotor		2.5–5
Disc brake caliper mount		5–7
Derailleur mounting (rear)		8–10
External bottom brackets		35–50
Freehub to hub		35–50
Headset		14.6–24.5
'Hollowtech II' crank arm pinch bolts		12–15
Pedals		29–40
Threadless steerer stem bolts		5–9
Saddle rail bolts	Single bolt	16–25
	2-bolt fixing	5–8
Seat-post clamp		4–6.8
Stem to handlebar bolts	1- or 2-bolt type	18–30
	4-bolt	4–8
Threadless stem	1- or 2-bolt	13.6–29.4
	4-bolt	5.4–16.3
	Fork column bolts	5–16.2
Quill stem		16.3–29.4
Quill stem expander wedge		20–25

Bottom bracket standards

BB standards have changed over recent years with BB30 and PF30 replacing 'threaded' as the most common. However, that's the tip of the BB iceberg as some bike manufacturers have created their own unique standards. Take the BBright Direct Fit and BB90, which are standards created to specifically fit Cervélo and Trek frames, respectively.

Type	Outside cup diameter	Inside diameter	Shell width
Threaded	35mm (36mm for Italian threading)	34mm (35mm for Italian threading)	68mm to 100mm
BB30	30mm spindle	42mm	68mm for road bikes; 73mm for mountain bikes
PF30	30mm spindle	46mm	68mm for road bikes; 73mm for mountain bikes
BB86 (for road bikes)	24mm spindle	41mm	86.5mm
BB92 (for mountain bikes)	24mm spindle	41mm	92mm
BB121	24mm spindle	41mm	121mm
BB90 and BB95 (Trek standards)	24mm spindle	37mm	90mm on road bikes; 95mm on mountain bikes
BBright Direct Fit (Cervélo standards)	30mm spindle	42mm	79mm
BBright Press Fit (Cervélo standards)	30mm spindle	46mm	79mm
386 Evo	30mm spindle	46mm	87mm

Headset standards

Like bottom brackets, headset standards have changed dramatically over the years. The industry noted this development and, in an attempt to clarify the situation, created a universal identification standard known as SHIS (Standardised Headset Identification System). As for abbreviations, EC stands for External Cup; ZS stands for Zero Stack; and IS stands for Integrated Headset.

Legacy name	SHIS	Cup OD (outside diameter)	Bore ID
1in JIS pressed cup	EC29	30mm	29.8–29.9
1-1/8in pressed cup	EC34	34	33.8–33.95
1in semi-integrated	ZS41	41.5	41.35–41.4
1-1/8in semi-integrated	ZS44	44.1	43.90–43.95
1-1/2in semi-integrated	ZS56	56	55.90–55.95
1in IS (Cane Creek)	IS38	38	38.15–38.25
1-1/8in IS (Cane Creek)	IS41	41	41.10–41.20
1-1/8in Italian (hiddenset)	IS42	41.8	41.95–42.05

Glossary

This section explains the meaning of terms commonly used by bike enthusiasts, including American words that have entered biking 'language' since the advent of mountain bikes.

Aerobars – Bars that extend from the front of your bike to improve aerodynamics. These come as all-in-one and fit onto your front steerer or clip on to your existing bars.

A-headset – Design of headset that dispenses with the traditional threaded steerer. Often referred to as 'Ahead', 'A'-head or 'threadless' steerer.

Allen key – A generic name for common six-sided hexagonal fitting and many head bolts. Technically Allen is a brand, and 'hex bolt' is the correct term.

Alloy – A mixture of metals and/or other elements that's usually better than a pure one.

Alloy rims – All decent-quality bikes have wheel rims made of aluminium alloy. Steel is the alternative material still to be found on cheaper bikes.

Anti-seize compound – A light grease containing powdered copper. The grease evaporates, leaving the copper behind which acts as a lubricant.

Axle – The central part of a bearing assembly. Many arguments take place as to the true definition of 'axle'. Some state that if it rotates then it's a spindle, if it's stationary and a component rotates around it then it's an axle.

Ball bearing – Usually means a hard-chromed, perfectly round steel ball that fits between the cup and cone in bike bearings. Also means the complete assembly of inner and outer race plus ball bearings, as used in a cartridge bottom bracket.

Bar ends – They look like cow horns bolted to the ends of straight handlebars. They provide an alternative hand position, especially useful for hill climbing or in traffic.

Bar-end shifters – Paddles at the end of aerobars that you shift to change up or down your gears. Helps to maintain aerodynamic position.

Battery – Seen on electric bikes and electronic groupsets. Both recharge via your mains but have differing battery lives.

Bead – The stiff edge of a tyre. Usually made of wire, but Kevlar is the usual choice for folding tyres.

Bearings – Any part designed to minimise the wear in a rotating or sliding assembly. On a bike the main bearings are the headset, bottom bracket and hub bearings.

Bottle boss – Threaded inserts used for attaching bottle cages and other items to the frame.

Bottom bracket – The bearings and spindle that carry the chainset.

Bottom bracket shell – The housing at the bottom of the seat and down tubes into which the bottom bracket is fitted.

Bracket-fit derailleur – A derailleur that fits directly into the drop out.

Brazed-on fitting – Items like bottle bosses and lever bosses attached permanently to the frame.

Butt – The thickened end of a tube.

Cable end-cap – A soft metal sleeve that can be crimped on to the end of a cable to prevent it fraying. Often simply called a 'cable crimp'.

Cable stop – A hollow tube brazed or welded on to the frame. The outer cable fits into the open end, while the inner cable passes out of the other. Often slotted so that you can pull the outer cable out, without disconnecting the inner one – useful when lubricating the inner cable.

Cantilever brakes – Attached to the frame via pivots on the fork blades and chain stays. Powerful brakes, fitted to most low-cost mountain bikes because mud doesn't build up around them. Also used on hybrids and tourers.

Carbon fibre – High-strength, relatively high-cost material used for making frames, seat posts and other components. The films are usually woven into a cloth or tape and bound together with resin. Very expensive and not suitable for everyday use.

Cartridge bottom bracket – A bottom bracket bearing in which the spindle runs on standard ball bearings, sealed inside a metal sleeve. Low maintenance. Becoming more and more popular.

Cassette – The common name for the rear block that doesn't contain the freewheel ratchet mechanism.

Centre-pull brakes – A brake with two separate arms independently mounted on a back plate.

Centre to centre – The traditional way of measuring frame size. It's the distance from the centre of the bottom bracket spindle to the seat post pinch bolt. No longer reliable in these days of compact frames.

Centring – Usually refers to adjusting the position of a brake in such a way that the brake pads are equally spaced from the braking surface. Can also refer to fitting a back wheel so that it's equally spaced between the chain stays.

Chain guard – Usually a light steel or plastic device that wraps around the chain, protecting the rider. Fixed to the frame with clips.

Chain line – This is the imaginary line between the front chain ring and the rear sprocket. A perfect chain line on a single-speed bike will have no sideways stress placed on the chain. On a derailleur-equipped bike the perfect chain line will run from the middle chain ring (on a triple chainset) to the middle sprocket on the rear cassette.

Chainring – The toothed part of the chainset that engages with the chain.

Chainset – The chainrings, spider and cranks are known collectively as the chainset.

Chain stay – The tube that runs between the bottom bracket and the drop out. It's usually oval near the bottom bracket.

Chamois pad – Good bike and bib shorts contain padding around the groin area for increased comfort.

Chrome molybdenum or chromoly – A steel alloy often used for bike frames. Though not a high-quality material, chrome molybdenum steel is ideal for budget-priced bikes.

Cleat – a moulded key that engages in the spring retention mechanism of a clipless pedal and is attached to the sole of the rider's shoe.

Clinchers – Detachable tyres that are held on to the wheel rim by stiff beads that clinch under the open edges of the rim.

Cluster – Usually short for sprocket cluster.

Cogs – People often speak of the chainring and sprockets as cogs because they're toothed. Not a correct use of the word.

Columbus – Italian maker of high-quality frame tubing.

Cotterless cranks – Cranks that bolt on to the square end of the bottom bracket spindle.

Cranks – Metal or carbon fibre components that carry the pedals and transmit the rider's energy to the chainrings.

Cup and cone bearing – The standard bike bearing assembly consisting of ball bearings trapped between the semi-circular cup and the tapered cone. These bearings are adjusted by moving the screwed part in or out until they turn freely, without any play.

Degreaser – Any solvent that will dissolve grease. Includes paraffin, diesel fuel and various specially formulated, ecologically acceptable brand-name products.

Derailleur – French word for gearing systems that work by 'derailing' the chain from one sprocket to another. Easily the most popular gearing system.

Diamond frame – The standard shape for a bike frame. Mountain bikes usually have a modified diamond frame.

Double-butted – Used to describe frame tubing which is drawn thin

in the middle for lightness and thicker at the ends where maximum strength is needed.

Down tube – Usually the largest-diameter part of the frame. Runs from the head tube to the bottom bracket.

Drop out – The part of the frame that carries the front or back wheel.

Dropper post – A seat post that can go up or down with a press of the button. Popular in mountain biking where steep descents are best managed with lower saddle height.

Drops – Short for drop handlebars found on racing and touring bikes.

Dual pivot brakes – A cross between side-pull and centre-pull brakes. More compact than centre-pulls and more powerful than side-pulls.

Electronic groupset – Groupset where traditional mechanical cable is replaced with electric current.

Expander bolt – A long bolt that fits into the upright part of the stem and screws into the cone or wedge that locks the stem into the frame.

Fixed wheel – A single sprocket screwed on to the rear hub, without a freewheel. All the time that the bike is moving, the rider has to pedal.

Fork crown – The top part of the forks. Sometimes it's separate, sometimes it's formed out of the fork blade itself.

Fork end – The part of the fork that carries the front wheel.

Forks – The steerable part of the frame that holds the front wheel.

Frame angles – The angle between the top tube and seat tube, and between the top tube and head tube. Greatly influences how the frame behaves on the road.

Freehub – A design of rear hub that has the sprocket cluster built in. Suitable for seven- or eight-speed set-ups, the right-hand hub bearing fits inside the cluster part.

Freewheel – Nearly all sprockets are mounted on a freewheel mechanism which allows you to coast along without pedalling.

Front mech – Short for 'front gear mechanism'. Alternatively called the front derailleur. Swaps the chain from one chainring to another. Two chainrings multiply the number of gears by two. Three chainrings multiply the number by three.

Gear hanger – The piece of metal that attaches the rear mech to the frame. Can be separate from, or part of, the frame.

Gear range – The gap between the lowest gear and the highest.

Gear ratio – On bikes, this is the distance that the bike will move for each revolution of the cranks – about 1m (40in) per revolution on a low gear, and around 2.7m (110in) on a high gear.

'Granny ring' – The low gear of a triple-ring chainset.

Hard-tail – A bike with no rear suspension.

Headset – The top and bottom bearings that support the forks and allow them to turn, thus providing steering. The bottom bearing is subject to very heavy loads and must be replaced when dents form in the bearing track.

Head tube – The shortest frame tube. Fits between the top and down tubes.

High gear – A gear ratio in which you travel a long way for every revolution of the cranks. In high, the chain is on the largest chainring and one of the smallest sprockets.

Hub gears – The alternative system to derailleur gears. Contained within an enlarged rear hub. Three, five, seven and fourteen-speed versions are now available.

Hybrid – A type of bike combining some mountain-bike components and frame features with large wheels and a fairly normal frame. Sometimes called city bikes.

Hydro-formed – Frame tubes manipulated into complex shapes under high pressure.

Indexed gears – Derailleur gears with a shifter that has click stops indicating each gear position.

Jockey wheels – Small wheels that guide the chain round the sprockets and towards the chainring

Kevlar – A high-strength artificial fibre used for reinforcing tyres and other components.

Knobblies – Deeply treaded tyres designed for high grip in mud.

Layback – The distance between the seat rail clamp and the centreline of the seat post tube.

Low gear – A gear ratio in which you move a short distance for every revolution of the cranks. Used for climbing hills and off-road.

Lube – Short for lubricant.

Lug – A complex steel sleeve used to join the main tubes of a frame.

Mech hanger – The mounting point for the rear derailleur. On steel and titanium frames this is often part of the rear drop out. On other frames the hanger is bolted on to the rear drop out and is replaceable.

Nipple – The metal nut that passes through the rim and screws on to the spoke. Spokes are tensioned by tightening the nipple.

Noodle – The short length of pipe that connects the brake cable to the brake on bikes fitted with V brakes.

Phillips screwdriver – A screwdriver with cross-shaped tip. Sizes 1 and 2 are both used on bikes and are not interchangeable.

Play – Unwanted movement in a bearing. Can be due to wear or incorrect adjustment.

Presta valve – Found mainly on racing bike tyres. Has a knurled section on the end to keep it closed.

Quick release – Usually refers to the mechanism that allows you to remove a bike wheel with just a turn of a lever. Can also refer to other quick release components like seat post clamps and panniers.

Quill stem – The traditional stem that's secured with an expanding wedge.

Race – Part of a bearing assembly in contact with the ball bearings.

Rear mech – Short for rear gear mechanism or rear derailleur. Deals with up to 11 sprockets.

Reynolds – British maker of high-quality steel tubing for frames.

Rim – The part of the wheel on which the tyre is mounted.

Roadster – Old-fashioned sit-up-and-beg bike.

Rotor – Or disc. The braking surface on disc brakes.

Sag – The distance the suspension compresses on a full suspension bike with the rider sat on board.

Schrader valve – Car-type tyre valve that has a separate insert. Larger in diameter than a Presta valve.

Seat post – The tube that fits into the seat tube and supports the saddle.

Seat stay – The small-diameter tube that runs between the seat lug and the drop out.

Seat tube – The large-diameter frame tube that supports the saddle.

700c tyre – The type of tyre normally fitted to good-quality road bikes. Thin, light and strong.

Shifter – Refers to any mechanism for changing gear.

Slicks – Smooth tyres used on mountain bikes for riding on the road.

Spider – The part of the drive-side crank arm that carries the chainrings. Most chainrings are mounted to either a four- or five-bolt crank arm spider.

Spoke – The thin wire component that connects the hub to the rim.

Spoke key – Spanner used to adjust the nipples that tension the spokes on a bicycle wheel.

Spray lube – Refers to various brands of silicon-based aerosol lubricant. Also to the specialist bike type, which contains a solid lubricant that remains after the liquid part has evaporated.

Sprints – A very light combination of wheels and tyres used solely for road and track racing. The tube is sewn into the tyre and the whole thing is then stuck to the rim.

Sprocket – The toothed wheel or wheels attached to the back wheel that transfer drive from the chain to the hub.

Sprocket cluster – Collective name for all the sprockets of a derailleur gear system.

Steerer tube – The tube that fits into the fork crown and is supported by the headset. Turns with the fork.

Stem – Fits into the steerer tube and supports the handlebars.

STI – A gear-changing system made by Shimano in which the shifters are built into the brake levers.

Straddle cable – A short cable that joins two independent brake arms. Found on some cantilever and all centre-pull brakes.

Suspension forks – Forks that allow the front wheel to move up and down to absorb bumps. The movement is usually controlled by some sort of spring and a gas or fluid damper mechanism.

Toe-in – Usually measured in millimetres. Refers to fitting brake pads closer to the rim at the front than at the back.

Top tube – The tube joining the seat tube to the head tube. It's usually horizontal, but increasing numbers of bikes have a sloping top tube.

Transmission – All the components that deal with transmitting power from the rider's legs to the back wheel. That means chainset, chain and sprockets, plus the front and rear mechs.

Travel – Often referred to the air or spring fork of mountain bikes, this refers to the amount of movement of a fork.

Tubeless – Where the inner tube is removed; instead, a deeper wheel rim and tighter fit means only a tyre is needed. Often contains sealant for puncture protection.

Tubeless pump – Pump that stores 'inflation' within a chamber. You then release a valve to 'pop inflate' the tubeless tyre onto the rim.

Tubulars – A tyre where the tube is sewn inside the tread part. Used with sprints.

Tyre valve – A device that holds air pressure in a tyre. On a bike the valve is actually part of the tube.

Tyre wall – Also referred to as the sidewall. The area of a tyre between the tread and the wheel rim. Sometimes a yellow colour that contrasts with the black of the tread.

V brake – The standard brake on mountain and commuter bikes. Developed by Shimano after the U brake – hence its name.

Wheel rim – The outer part of a bike wheel that carries the tyre. Also the braking surfaces. Can be made of steel or other alloys.

Wheel well – The centre part of the rim, where the spokes sit.

Wireless – Most bike computers measure speed wirelessly via a sensor on the fork sending a signal to the head unit. Sram's electronic groupset is also wireless.

Wishbone stay – A design of chain stay in which the two tubes join above the back wheel and are connected to the seat cluster by a larger single tube.

Index

Written by:	James Witts & Mark Storey
Copy editor:	Ian Heath
Technical reader:	Chaz Curry
Studio photography:	Paul Buckland
Mechanic:	Jonny Ashelford
Illustrations:	Ian Bott
Page design:	James Robertson & Christopher Borgman
Project manager:	Louise McIntyre

In addition, the author and publisher would like to thank the many
manufacturers and suppliers who provided bikes, components, tools,
pictures and information to help in the creation of this book.

First published 1994
Second edition published 1995
Third edition published 1999
Reprinted 2000 (with minor amendments)
Reprinted 2002
Fourth edition piblished 2003
Reprinted 2003, 2004, 2005 and 2006
Fifth edition published 2007
Reprinted 2008, 2009 (twice), 2010 and 2011 (twice)
Sixth edition published May 2012
Reprinted 2013, 2014 and 2015 (twice)
Seventh edition published April 2017

A catalogue record for this book is available from the British Library.

ISBN 978 1 78521 134 8

Published by Haynes Publishing
Sparkford, Yeovil, Somerset BA22 7JJ, UK

Tel: 01963 440635
Int. tel: +44 1963 440635
Website: www.haynes.com

Printed in Malaysia.